Chalet Cookbook One

Straightforward recipes for chalet hosts

Dev Jaffe

Mountainsun France

Copyright © 2017 Dev Jaffe

All rights reserved.

ISBN: 1974028917
ISBN-13: 9781974028917

CHAPTER HEADINGS

1	Colour codes and Chapter Index	1
2	Breakfast	7
3	Cakes and Cookies	13
4	Children's Options	26
5	Soups and Starters	31
6	Meat and Fish Mains	40
7	Vegetarian Mains	50
8	Vegetables, Sides and Sauces	57
9	Salads	63
10	Desserts	66

PREFACE

I have more than 25 years of experience cooking, menu planning and training for ski chalets. The bottom-line is that everyone is working to a budget but that does vary hugely from company to company. Many kitchens are tiny and often open to your guests, so your organisation and kitchen hygiene are on display. Often you will be tired and maybe cooking isn't the top of your list for either early morning or after a great day on the mountain BUT it must be done well and you will get most out of your season and your guests if you look after them as you would your own mum. Your guests deserve the holiday of a lifetime and your food is a key part of their experience.

The recipes in this book are hassle free, work at altitude, work in small kitchens and have great feedback from our own guests at Mountainsun. The recipes either assume you have access to a food processor, mixer etc. or if you are extremely lucky and have forward thinking chalet owners, a Thermomix. Most recipes have 'free from' alternatives as more and more people with dietary requirements seem to be hitting the slopes – they will be so delighted and relieved to discover that they will not have to spend all their week eating salad and shop bought tasteless GF cookies.

For you to maximise your snow time it is essential to be really organised. Routines and lists may seem a drag but they will allow you to have a great season. Working and eating a weekly menu may seem a bit boring but it will become automatic (very useful if you have over indulged a bit) and the best way to stick to your budget.

When you are planning your menu think texture, colour and taste. Spiced butternut squash soup, butter chicken curry and saffron rice pudding – NO – all too similar texture, theme and colour – not to mention porridge at breakfast and orange yogurt cake for tea, see what I mean?

Think guests, how does your menu fit with where they are in their holiday – their appetites will grow during the week, believe me. Guests may have had a very early start to get to you and then struggled a bit with travel sickness so the first night, help their stomachs with safe food. Soup is great for first night and maybe for some guests that is all they will manage. Easy to eat things like lasagna with a salad aren't too heavy on the system and then a light fruit based dessert finishes the meal off sympathetically. Also, think about preparing a meal for change over day that is both straight forward to prepare ahead of time and easy to reheat for late arrivals.

Think best use of your budget both money and time. If you're making meringue for pavlova, then make more mix at the same time and cook small meringues for a teatime option for later in the week. Use the spare egg yolks in the spice cookie recipe so nothing is wasted and sausages of cookie dough are now sitting in your freezer waiting to be sliced and baked – please note that latest regulations in France do not let you freeze spare portions etc. so check first.

For most recipes, I have included as many Dairy Free, Gluten Free and Low Carb-Healthy Fat (DF/GF/LCHF) alternatives as are straightforward to do. Note though that some of the alternatives will cost you significantly more such as using an avocado half to replace a bun or ground almonds instead of flour.

This cook book is both easy to use and packed full of ideas to help you through your season. I have colour-coded the chapters, recipe alternatives, tips and hints for ease of use. Have fun cooking in the mountains.

COLOUR CODES

- USEFUL TIPS AND HINTS
- FREE FROM
- VARIATIONS
- BREAKFAST
- CAKES AND COOKIES
- CHILDREN'S OPTIONS
- SOUPS AND STARTERS
- MAINS
- VEGETARIAN MAINS
- VEGETABLES, SIDES AND SAUCES
- SALADS
- DESSERTS

RECIPES BY SECTION

BREAKFAST

BREAKFAST QUANTITIES	7
CHEESY EGGS	8
EGGS BENEDICT: FLORENTINE OR ROYALE	9
EGGY BREAD	12
FLORENTINE SCRAMBLE	8
LCHF PANCAKES	12
OMELETTES	10
PORRIDGE	12
SCRAMBLED EGGS	8
THICK PANCAKES/DROP SCONES	11
THIN PANCAKES	11

CAKES AND COOKIES

ANOTHER QUICK YOGURT CAKE	14
BASIC SPONGE CAKES – VICTORIA, COFFEE AND BERRY	17
CARROT CAKE	15
CHOCOLATE CHIP COOKIES	21
CHOCOLATE MUD CAKE	18
CHRISTMAS GINGERBREAD	23
CLASSIC SKI CHALET YOGURT CAKE	14
COURGETTE, LIME AND POPPYSEED CAKE	16
FLAPJACKS	20
GF ORANGE/LEMON POLENTA CAKE	25

GF PASTRY	25
GF/DF COCONUT MACAROONS	24
GF/DF SPANISH ALMOND CAKE	24
GINGER COOKIES	22
MINCE PIES	23
SCONES	20
SHORTBREAD	22
SPEEDY MOUNTAIN FRUIT CAKE	19
SPICED BISCUITS	21

CHILDREN'S OPTIONS

BAKED CHICKEN OR FISH GOUJONS	29
CHEESE AND HAM POTATO BAKE	27
CHICKEN STIR FRY	28
CREAMY CHICKEN AND LEEKS	28
JACKETS	27
TUNA, BROCCOLI AND PASTA BAKE	29

SOUPS AND STARTERS

ALL IN ONE MUSHROOM SOUP	33
BAKED CAMEMBERT	38
BRIE EN CROUTE	38
BRUSCHETTA	39
BUTTERNUT SQUASH/PUMPKIN SOUP	32
CHRISTMAS OR SPECIAL OCCASION SMOKED SALMON PATE	36
CREAMY ZUCCHINI SOUP	33
HERBY CREAM CHEESE BALLS	36
GOAT'S CHEESE, WALNUT AND SUNDRIED TOMATO TART	37

LEMON TUNA PATE	35
MELBA TOAST	36
MUSHROOM PATE	35
SPICED LENTIL AND TOMATO SOUP	34
SPINACH SOUP	31
VEGETABLE SOUP	32
WILD MUSHROOM TARTS	37

MAINS

BEEF AND BEER PIE	42
CHICKEN AND MUSHROOM PIE	42
DUCK CASSOULET	44
FISH PIE	48
HERB CRUSTED SALMON	49
ITALIAN BEEF CASSEROLE	47
LASAGNE	41
MEDITTERANEAN LAMB	46
MINCE AND VEGETABLES PIE	43
PARMESAN CHICKEN	45
PORK FILLET MIGNON IN HONEY MUSTARD SAUCE	46
ROASTED PEPPER, MOZZARELLA AND BASIL STUFFED CHICKEN	45
STICKY GINGER CHICKEN	44
TARTIFLETTE	40

VEGETARIAN MAINS

BAKED AUBERGINE MELTS	50
CELEBRATION NUT ROAST	56
COURGETTES WITH GINGER AND GARLIC SAUCE	53
ITALIAN STUFFED PEPPERS	50
LENTIL AND VEGETABLE STEW	54
MUSHROOM PANCAKES	51
NUTTY RISSOLES	51
ROAST VEGETABLE CASSOULET	52
SPINACH AND MUSHROOM LASAGNE	55
VEGETABLE GRATIN	56
WILD MUSHROOM TARTIFLETTE	53

VEGETABLES, SIDES AND SAUCES

BALSAMIC REDUCTION	60
BOULANGERE POTATOES	59
CARAMELIZED ONIONS	61
DAUGHINOISE POTATOES	59
HASSELBACK POTATOES	59
PICANTE SAUCE	62
QUANTITIES OF VEGETABLES	57
RED PEPPER JAM	60
RED PEPPER SAUCE	61
WAYS OF TARTING UP VEGETABLES	57

SALADS

CAESAR SALAD	64
FOUR SEASONS SALAD	64
GOAT'S CHEESE SALAD	65
GREEK SALAD	65
NICOISE SALAD	63

DESSERTS

CARAMELIZED BANANAS	70
CHOCOLATE ORANGE MOUSSE	69
CHOCOLATE PEARS	70
CHOCOLATE SAUCE	70
CRÈME BRULEE	67
CUSTARD	74
DAME BLANCHE	70
EMERGENCY DESSERT	66
FROZEN FRUIT SORBET	72
FRUIT CRUMBLE	73
FRUIT TART	69
FRUIT TRIFLE	74
LEMON TART	68
PANNA COTTA	71
PAVLOVA	66
STICKY TOFFEE PUDDING AND SAUCE	71
TIRAMISU	72

2 BREAKFAST

Plan your breakfast options carefully. Breakfast day one needs to be gentle as some guests may be over tired as they are not yet used to their chalet bed. They are stressed because they may be a bit nervous and if they have kids with them - well use your imagination. Scrambled eggs are easy to make and easy to eat, save your 'show off' options like Eggs Benedict for later in the week when your guests will really appreciate them.

Many people become dehydrated in the mountains so always have a jug of water out with the fruit juice. This will help your budget as water is free and juice is not. If you offer meats and cheeses try to provide a variety e.g. day one is ham and day two is salami for example. It is all too easy to expect that your fellow chalet hosts will know what has been served the day before, so make a weekly list and then stick to it. Ideally, you'll have prepped the meat and cheese slices the evening before (but check local regulations) so all you need to do in the morning is present them appetisingly and remember to provide a fork or tongs to serve them with.

Find a tactful way of reminding guests that the food you offer them is for breakfast and not their packed lunches or else watch your costs start to increase.

Maybe a last thing to think about at breakfast is clearing away as guests come and go. Nobody wants to sit on someone else's crumbs.

BREAKFAST QUANTITIES

Guessing quantities is always tricky but if you pay attention to your guests early in their stay that should help you adjust portion sizes. This table is a very rough guide to help with your food ordering.

Number guests	6	12	18	24
Boiled, fried or poached Eggs	9	18	27	36
Croissant or Pain au chocolate	9	18	27	36
Sausage (normal size) or double if chipolata size	6	12	18	24
Fried/grilled tomato	6	12	18	24
Pancetta to wrap tomato (slice)	12	24	36	48
Tomato (halved)	6	12	18	24
Bacon slice	12	24	36	48
Baked beans (g)	600	1200	1800	2400

And remember to season: salt, pepper and herbs all work well for breakfast options

SCRAMBLED EGGS

Number guests	6	12	18	24
Eggs	12	24	36	48
Cream/milk (g)	150	300	450	600

Small quantities

1. **Whisk** together eggs, milk, s/p
2. **Heat** butter in pan and cook
3. **Keep warm** over water bath or in hotplate

Large quantities

1. **Oven** at 350/180/4
2. **Add** butter into large pan in oven to melt
3. **Whisk** together eggs, milk, s/p
4. **Pour** egg mix into melted butter cook 10 mins
5. **Remove** from oven and stir eggs
6. **Bake** further 15-20 mins until eggs just set

CHEESY EGGS

Number guests	6	12	18	24
Eggs	8	16	24	32
Cream/milk (g)	100	200	300	400
Grated cheese (g)	100	200	300	400

1. Follow instructions as above adding grated cheese when mixing together eggs and milk

FLORENTINE SCRAMBLE

Number guests	6	12	18	24
Eggs	8	16	24	32
Cream/milk (g)	100	200	300	400
Chopped onion	1	2	3	4
Chopped garlic	1	2	3	4
Sliced mushrooms (g)	100	200	300	400
Frozen spinach (g)	200	400	600	800
Cherry tomatoes halved	10	20	30	40

1. **Fry** onions and garlic until soft
2. **Add** mushrooms, spinach and tomatoes
3. **Add** to egg mix before cooking

DF   Use alternative to milk and cook in oil

EGGS BENEDICT: FLORENTINE OR ROYALE

Number guests	6	12	18	24
Hollandaise				
Egg yolks	4	8	14	16
Butter (g), cubed	130	260	390	520
Lemon juice	½	1	1.5	2
Hot water	15	30	45	60
Eggs	6	12	18	24
Muffin/roll	3	6	9	12
Slice ham	6	12	18	24
Slice smoked salmon	6	12	18	24
Slice speck	12	24	36	48
Spinach (g)	300	600	900	1200

HOLLANDAISE – USE THERMOMIX

1. Insert butterfly whisk
2. Add all ingredients to the bowl cook 4 mins/80/Sp3
3. Repeat cooking in two-minute intervals until sauce is thick

HOLLANDAISE – MICROWAVE

1. Beat egg yolks, lemon juice, hot water and seasoning together in a microwave-safe bowl until smooth.
2. Slowly drizzle melted butter into the egg yolk mixture while continually whisking.
3. Heat in microwave for 15 to 20 seconds; whisk. Repeat till sauce thickens

If sauce separates, add an ice cube and whisk until combined.
If sauce fails to thicken add an extra egg yolk (sometimes the lemon is too acid), mix and cook again.

BENEDICT: FLORENTINE, ROYALE

1. Poach eggs
2. Serve on half a toasted roll or muffin, either sliced ham or smoked salmon or speck or spinach, then poached egg and cover with Hollandaise.
3. For Eggs Florentine, cook and drain frozen spinach before serving

DF Use a DF spread instead of butter
GF Serve with GF roll
LCHF Serve on avocado half

OMELETTES

Number guests	6	12	18	24
Eggs	12	24	36	48
CHEESE				
Grated cheese (g)	100	200	300	400
MUSHROOM				
Sliced mushrooms (g)	400	800	1200	1600
TOMATO & BASIL				
Tomatoes (chopped)	6	12	18	24
Basil leaves (chopped)	20	40	60	80
SPANISH				
Cooked chopped potato (g)	300	600	900	1200
Sliced onion	1	2	3	4
Parsley chopped (g)	5	10	15	20

1. **Small numbers: cook omelettes individually**
2. **Large numbers: cook in a large frying pan and serve in wedges**

Cheese

3. Gently beat eggs together and season
4. Heat butter in frying pan until foaming
5. Add eggs to pan and cook till lightly set, keep pushing uncooked parts to the centre of the pan.
6. When eggs have just set but are still soft add the cheese and cook till melted
7. Fold the omelette in half and serve

Mushroom

1. Fry mushrooms in butter
2. Gently beat eggs together and season
3. Add eggs to mushroom pan and cook till lightly set, keep pushing uncooked parts to the centre of the pan.
4. When omelette is set fold in half and serve

Tomato and Basil

1. As for mushroom but replace mushrooms with tomatoes and basil in step 1

Spanish

1. As for mushroom but replace mushrooms with onions in step 1
2. Add potatoes and parsley with eggs at step 3

DF   Cook omelette in oil
LCHF   Replace potatoes with courgettes in Spanish Omelette

THICK PANCAKES/DROP SCONES – 1 per guest

Number guests	6	12	18	24
Butter (g)	50	100	150	200
Eggs	2	4	6	8
Milk (g)	300	600	900	1200
Sugar (g)	30	60	90	120
Flour (g)	200	400	600	800
Baking Powder (g)	15	30	45	60
Salt (tsp)	.25	.5	.75	1
Frozen berries (g)	30	60	90	120
Bananas	2	4	6	8
Cocoa (g)	5	10	15	20

Thermomix method
1. **Melt** butter in Thermomix **2min/70/1**
2. **Add** remaining ingredients mix 10s/5

Microwave method
1. **Melt** butter in microwave
2. **Whisk** eggs till light and fluffy
3. **Add** other ingredients and whisk till smooth

Fry pancakes in very hot well-greased pan

Chocolate	Add cocoa at Step 2
Berries or bananas	Add berries or bananas to batter whilst cooking

DF Replace milk and butter with non-dairy alternatives
GF Use GF flour or below LCHF recipe

THIN PANCAKES – 2 per guest

Number guests	6	12	18	24
Flour (g)	250	500	750	1000
Eggs	2	4	6	8
Milk (g)	500	1000	1500	2000
Salt (tsp)				

1. Whisk all ingredients together until smooth or mix in Thermomix 20s/6

LCHF – PANCAKES (GF)

Number guests	6
Ground Almonds (g)	150
Eggs	6
Cream cheese (g)	350
Baking Powder (g)	15
Vanilla (tsp)	2

1. Mix all ingredients till smooth
2. Fry in well-buttered pan

EGGY BREAD / FRENCH TOAST

Number guests	6	12	18	24
Slices bread	12	24	36	48
Eggs	6	12	18	24
Milk (g)	250	500	750	1000

1. Mix eggs and milk together
2. Dip bread into egg mix
3. Fry till golden in butter

CINNAMON SUGAR - Make up a large jar using following ration 200g sugar: 15g cinnamon

Some people like their eggy bread sweet, others savoury so maybe have golden syrup, cinnamon sugar and ketchup available

PORRIDGE

Number guests	6	12	18	24
Oats (g)	300	600	900	1200
Milk/water (l)	2	4	6	8

1. Cook and stir till thickened

Different oats need different quantities of liquid (milk, milk/water or just water). Experiment to see what yours need. For faster cooking soak the oats the night before.

DF Use coconut milk

Add spices and/or dried fruit

3 AFTERNOON TEA

My belief is that afternoon tea is one of the most important chalet meals. How lovely to return to the chalet and be met by a luscious looking cake or plate of homemade cookies. Good teatime treats make guests feel very much at home and looked after. They also fill up the guests in a very economical way so they won't be starving at dinner time. For me, yoghurt cake seven ways doesn't cut it and there is no excuse when other recipes are so quick and easy. You want your guests licking their lips in anticipation on their last run down and that won't happen if they get the same texture cake but a different artificial flavour each day. I'm not anti the classic mountain chalet quick yoghurt cake just not every day. Guests remember great cakes – it's true!

Getting the quantities of cake or cookies needed can be tricky. Some guests grab the first lifts, ski hard till last lift and have only stopped for a rapid toilet stop. They will arrive back to the chalet seriously hungry knowing that there will be free cake to grab. Others have long leisurely lunches or are watching their figures so may select a delicate slice. And if there are children staying you can be cleared out very fast. Some companies provide lovely fresh bread, butter and jam and although it will become crumb city, fewer cakes then get demolished.

Presenting your cakes attractively takes seconds but has the wow effect. A dusting of icing sugar, a doily, feather icing or some fresh berries makes all the difference. Some hosts pre-slice their cakes others leave them whole. In the spring, you may acquire flies as they awaken so make sure your cakes are protected. Lastly, if you are using a whipped cream filling don't leave your luscious cake out all day as it may go off quite fast, save the cream filling cake for the day you are around at tea time and can serve straight from the cold room/fridge.

Many guests now want GF and or DF food. There are lots of easy recipes although many use ground almonds which are of course is more expensive than flour. It is incredibly annoying to have spent the time making something special for your GF guest only to discover they ate pasta on the mountain for lunch! Those guests with Celiac disease are different and you need to pay attention to keep their food well away from anything with gluten but it never fails to amaze me how many GF guests love a good piece of Victoria sponge and a pint of beer!

The recipes provide for very generous portions. It's always useful to have some extra cake around either to top up or entertain unexpected guests like the resort manager or landlady. And worst-case scenario make trifle. In countries where you are allowed to freeze cooked cake, a great use of time is to double bake and freeze one cake un-iced.

CLASSIC SKI CHALET YOGURT CAKE

You can vary the cake by using pre-flavoured yoghurts or if you use natural yoghurt as the base you can just play and add what you like for example coffee, cocoa, desiccated coconut and cherries. The cakes will all look different, have a different flavour but they all will have a distinctive texture.

ALL MEASUREMENTS IN YOGURT POTS – so easy a five-year-old can make it

Number guests	6	12	18	24
Yogurt small pot	1	2	3	4
Oil	1	2	3	4
Sugar	2	4	6	8
Eggs	3	6	9	12
SR Flour	3	6	9	12

1. Oven 160, line cake tins (works well in loaf tin)
2. Mix all ingredients together in Thermomix 30s/sp 6 or mix in food mixer or by hand
3. Cook 25-30 mins

ANOTHER QUICK YOGURT CAKE FOR A BIT OF VARIETY

Number guests	6	12	18	24
Yogurt small pot	1	2	3	4
Sugar (g)	100	200	300	400
Eggs	1	2	3	4
SR Flour (g)	100	200	300	400
VARIATIONS				
Orange or lemon peel	1	2	3	4
Frozen berries	50	10	150	200
Choc chip	50	10	150	200

1. Oven 160, line cake tins (works well in loaf tin)
2. Mix all ingredients together in Thermomix 30s/sp 6 or mix in food mixer or by hand
3. Cook 25-30 mins

If using orange or lemon, first chop peel into sugar 30s/Sp7 before adding other ingredients

If using berries or chocolate, stir in by hand after mixing ingredients

DF   Use DF yoghurts like soya

CARROT CAKE

Number guests	6	12	18	24
Oil (g)	100	200	300	400
Brown Sugar (g)	100	200	300	400
Eggs	2	4	6	8
Carrots in chunks(g)	250	500	750	1000
SR Flour (g)	200	400	600	800
Mixed spice (g)	5	10	15	20
Salt (tsp)	.5	1	1.5	2
Icing				
Mascarpone/ cr. cheese (g)	100	200	300	400
Icing sugar (g)	250	500	750	1000
Orange peel	.5	1	1.5	2

1. Oven 160, line tins
2. **Thermomix method**

Combine all ingredients 45s/sp6, scrape down repeat for another 20s if mixture not smooth enough

Non-Thermomix method
3. Grate carrots and set aside
4. Whisk oil and sugar together
5. Whisk in eggs till well combined
6. Stir in grated carrots, flour and spices
7. Cook 45min – I hr

For topping Thermomix method
8. grind orange peel and icing sugar 30s/Sp8
9. Add cream cheese mix 30s/sp 6

For topping Non-Thermomix method
10. Zest orange
11. Combine zest, icing sugar and cream cheese till smooth

Add dried fruit or nuts to the mix before cooking

DF – if you leave off the icing (you could make the icing and leave in a bowl by the cake for the guests to help themselves)

COURGETTE, LIME AND POPPYSEED CAKE

Number guests	6	12	18	24
Oil (g)	80	160	240	320
Sugar (g)	100	200	300	400
Eggs	2	4	6	8
Courgettes in chunks(g)	150	300	450	60
SR Flour (g)	150	300	450	60
Baking powder (g)	5	10	15	20
Lime zest	1	2	3	4
Poppy seeds (g)	5	10	15	20
Icing				
Mascarpone/ cr. cheese (g)	100	200	300	400
Icing sugar (g)	250	500	750	1000
Lime juice (lime)	1	2	3	4

1. Oven 160, line cake tins

Thermomix method

2. Grind lime peel and sugar 30s/sp8
3. Add all other ingredients and mix 20 s/sp6, scrape down and mix 10s/sp6

Non-Thermomix method

4. Grate courgettes and set aside
5. Whisk oil and sugar together
6. Whisk in eggs till well combined
7. Stir in grated courgettes, flour, baking powder, lime zest and poppy seeds

8. Bake 40 – 50 mins
9. Mix all icing ingredients 30s/Sp 6 in Thermomix or by hand

DF leave off the icing (you could make the icing and leave in a bowl by the cake for the guests to help themselves)

VANILLA SUGAR

Make a large jar and use to flavour cakes instead of vanilla essence. Use 1 vanilla pod to 250g sugar. Keep topping up the sugar as you use it until vanilla pod stops flavouring the sugar

BASIC SPONGE CAKES – VICTORIA - COFFEE - BERRY

ALL IN ONE SPONGE CAKES – they do work in the mountains!

Number guests	6	12	18	24
Soft Butter (g)	100	200	300	400
Sugar (g)	100	200	300	400
Eggs	2	4	6	8
Milk (g)	30	60	90	120
SR Flour (g)	100	200	300	400
Baking powder (g)	5	10	15	20
VARIATIONS				
Vanilla essence (tsp)	1	2	3	4
Coffee (g)	30	60	90	120
Walnuts (g)	20	40	60	80
Frozen fruit (g)	100	200	300	400
Filling				
Cream (g)	250	500	750	1000
Frozen fruit (g)	100	200	300	400
Coffee (g)	30	60	90	120
Butter (g)	50	100	150	200
Icing sugar (g)	75	150	225	300
Vanilla essence (tsp)	1	2	3	4
Jam (g)	100	200	300	400

1. Oven 180, line cake rounds

Thermomix method

2. Mix together sugar, butter, flour, baking powder, vanilla essence, milk and eggs 15-20 s/sp 6 **DON'T OVERMIX**
3. **Non-Thermomix method**
4. **Whisk together** sugar, butter, flour, baking powder, vanilla essence, milk and eggs till smooth
5. For **Fruit sponge** stir in frozen fruit by hand when other ingredients mixed
6. For **Coffee sponge** replace milk with cold strong coffee
7. Bake in lined tins 20-30 mins depending on thickness

Fillings

1. **Fruit sponge** fill with whipped cream and berries, dust top with icing sugar
2. For **Victoria sponge** make butter cream filling by mixing butter, icing sugar and vanilla essence Thermomix 30s/Sp 5 or with mixer, spread a layer of jam on cake, top with butter cream, dust top with icing sugar
3. For **Coffee sponge** make double the recipe butter cream with coffee instead of essence, spread in centre of cake and top, decorate with walnuts

CHOCOLATE MUD CAKE

A rich dense cake that is very filling

Number guests	6	12	18	24
CAKE				
Chocolate white, milk or dark (g)	75	150	225	300
Butter (g)	125	250	375	500
Sugar (g)	200	400	600	800
Milk (g)	125	250	375	500
Flour (g)	125	250	375	500
SR Flour (g)	25	50	75	100
Eggs – lightly beaten	1	2	3	4
Vanilla Essence (tsp)	1	2	3	4
GANACHE ICING				
Cream (ml or g)	75	150	225	300
Chocolate white, milk or plain (g)	150	300	450	600

1. Oven 160 and line round tins for small quantities, oven trays for large quantities
2. For 6 or 12 weigh chocolate, butter, sugar and milk into Thermomix, melt 5 min/70/sp3. Without a Thermomix melt in saucepan as for larger quantities
3. When melted mix in remaining ingredients, Thermomix 15s/sp5 or by stick blender/hand in saucepan
4. Pour into the lined tins and bake 45min -1hr, check and then lightly cover with foil and continue baking till cooked
5. While cake is cooking or cooling make topping
6. Small quantities in Thermomix heat cream 2min/90/sp2, add chocolate and stir speed 2 until melted
7. Without a Thermomix or for large quantities boil cream in a saucepan and then stir in weighed chocolate to melt

ONLY add topping to cake when cake completely cool or icing will not have a smooth finish

Add frozen raspberries or strawberries to a white chocolate mud cake

Add orange zest to a dark chocolate mud cake

Make a white and dark chocolate mix and combine as for a marble cake

SPEEDY MOUNTAIN FRUIT CAKE

> This cake keeps really well wrapped in foil so make more than you need and store for another time. If you make packed lunches for guests then a hunk of this cake goes so well with their sandwiches.

Hopefully you will be provided with a Christmas cake already made, maybe even marzipanned and iced. If not and it's a last-minute panic bake this cake and drench with some brandy after its cooled and before icing. Also, would work as an Easter cake for those of you have a longer season.

Number guests	6	12	18	24
Mixed dried fruit (g)	500	1000	1500	2000
Condensed milk can (400g)	1/2	1	1.5	2
SR flour (g)	200	400	600	800
Mixed spice (tsp)	1	2	3	4
Eggs	1	2	3	4

1. Oven 150, line baking tray or round
2. Put a little water and dried fruit in saucepan and heat to moisten fruit for 5 minutes (you could also use black tea or brandy)
3. Stir in remaining ingredients
4. Cook 1 – 1 and half hours

Add nuts or seeds to the mix

Change mixed spice for cinnamon

FLAPJACKS

Number guests	6	12	18	24
Butter (g)	125	250	375	500
Demerara Sugar (g)	175	350	525	700
Oats (g)	200	400	600	800

1. Oven 140, line tin
2. Melt butter and sugar together until gloopy
3. Add oats
4. Cook till golden approx. 20 – 40 mins
5. Cut into portions before cooled

Add dried fruit
Add mixed spice
Add desiccated coconut

GF   apart from for Celiacs as the oats aren't 100% GF

SCONES - Need eating on the day!

Number guests	6	12	18	24
Butter (g)	75	150	225	300
Sugar (g)	50	100	150	200
Milk(g)	150	300	450	600
Flour (g)	300	600	900	1200
Baking powder (tsp)	2	4	6	8

1. Oven 220, line tray

Thermomix method

2. Knead all ingredients 20s, scrape down sides and repeat for 10s

Non-Thermomix method

3. Use food processor or rub in by hand - butter, sugar, flour and baking powder till breadcrumb texture
4. Stir in milk
5. Gently flatten, cut into rounds and bake 10-15 mins until golden

Add dried fruit at second knead OR Replace sugar with grated cheese

GF   use GF flour and baking powder

DF   use Non-dairy spread

SPICED BISCUITS – in the freezer backup cookies

Number guests	6	12	18	24
BASIC BISCUIT MIX				
Soft Butter (g)	125	250	375	500
Sugar (g)	125	250	375	500
Egg yolks	2	4	6	8
Flour (g)	200	400	600	800
VARIATIONS				
Cinnamon or mixed spice (tsp)	1	2	3	4
Dried fruit (g)	50	100	150	200
Chopped glace cherries (g)	50	100	150	200
Sliced almonds (g)	50	100	150	200
Christmas mincemeat (g)	50	100	150	200

1. Mix all biscuit ingredient together in Thermomix 30s/Sp6 or in Food processor
2. Add filling to mix and roll into 5cm sausages, wrap in cling-film and refrigerate OR freeze for future use
3. When the mix is chilled, cut into 3mm slices and place on lined tray
4. Bake 8-10 mins at 200

CHOCOLATE CHIP COOKIES – everyone's favourites

Number guests	6	12	18	24
Butter (g)	125	250	375	500
Demerara Sugar (g)	175	350	525	700
Eggs	1	2	3	4
SR Flour (g)	200	400	600	800
Milk (g)	15	30	45	60
Vanilla essence (tsp)	1	2	3	4
Chocolate chips (g)	250	500	750	1000

1. Oven 180, line trays with greaseproof paper
2. Smaller quantities in Thermomix: mix together all ingredients (APART from chocolate chips) Sp6/20s, scrape down and repeat if necessary or use food processor
3. Stir in choc chips Reverse/speed 4 until combined OR stir in by hand
4. Large quantities use Kitchen mixer OR make batches using Thermomix
5. Put large teaspoon size portions well spread out on trays
6. Bake approx. 15 mins

Use different types of chocolate, add nuts and/or dried fruit

SHORTBREAD

Number guests	6	12	18	24
Rice (g)	50	100	150	200
Butter (g)	200	400	600	800
Sugar (g)	125	250	375	500
Flour (g)	250	500	750	1000

1. Oven 150, line baking trays
2. Grind rice in Thermomix 1min/10 or grind in food processor
3. Add all ingredients in Thermomix mix 30s/5 or in food processor until mixed
4. Flatten mix into baking tray, score into squares, prick with fork
5. Bake 30 – 45 mins till golden

Add chocolate drops

GINGER COOKIES

Number guests	6	12	18	24
Butter (g)	125	250	500	750
Golden syrup (g)	60	125	250	500
Sugar (g)	60	125	250	500
SR flour (g)	250	500	750	1000
Bicarb (tsp)	1	2	3	4
Ginger (tsp)	2	4	6	8

1. Oven 180, line trays
2. In a saucepan melt butter, sugar and syrup together
3. Stir in dry ingredients
4. Put teaspoon size balls onto trays and bake 10 – 15 minutes until golden

Add chopped glace cherries

CHRISTMAS BAKING

GINGERBREAD COOKIES

Number guests	6	12	18	24
Butter (g)	125	250	500	750
Treacle (g)	30	60	90	120
Golden syrup (g)	30	60	90	120
Brown sugar (g)	125	250	500	750
Orange juice (tsp)	1	2	3	4
SR flour (g)	250	500	750	1000
Ginger (tsp)	2	4	6	8
Mixed spice (tsp)	1	2	3	4
Cinnamon (tsp)	1	2	3	4

1. Oven 180   line tray
2. Combine all ingredients in Thermomix or Food processor
3. Roll on floured board and cut out shapes
4. Bake 20 mins until golden

MINCE PIES

Number guests	6	12	18	24
SWEET PASTRY				
Icing sugar (g)	100	200	300	400
Butter (g)	250	500	750	1000
Flour (g)	350	700	1050	1400
Egg yolks	3	6	9	12
FILLINGS				
Mincemeat (g)	150	300	450	600

1. Oven 180 and lightly grease patty tin
2. In Thermomix or food processor chop butter, flour and icing sugar until mixture looks like breadcrumbs
3. Add egg yolks and mix few seconds until mixture JUST coming together
4. Tip pastry out, wrap in cling-film and place in fridge for an hour before rolling out (can freeze at this stage for later use)
5. Roll out and cut out rounds, push down in patty tin and add a spoonful of mincemeat Cut out smaller circles or stars to top
6. Bake 15 – 20 mins
7. Dust with icing sugar to serve

GF   Use GF pastry see page 27

FREE FROM CAKES AND COOKIES

Having a batch of coconut macaroons or meringues safely stored in a box is a great back up for those guests who forgot to tell you they were GF and/or DF. If they are only GF then you could sandwich meringues together with whipped cream for a bit of variety or even drizzle each meringue with chocolate.

COCONUT MACAROONS GF/DF (ALSO SEE MERINGUE RECIPE UNDER DESSERTS)

Number guests	6	12	18	24
Desiccated coconut (g)	200	400	600	800
Sugar (g)	125	250	375	500
Egg whites	2	4	6	8

1. Oven 150, line tray
2. Whisk egg whites till stiff
3. Stir in sugar and coconut
4. Place dessert spoonfuls on tray and place half a glace cherry on top to decorate (optional)
5. Bake till golden, 15-25 mins

SPANISH ORANGE ALMOND CAKE GF/DF

Number guests	6	12	18	24
Ground almonds (g)	250	500	750	1000
Sugar (g)	250	500	750	1000
Eggs	4	8	12	16
Orange peel	1	2	3	4

1. Oven 160, Line cake tin

Thermomix method

2. Grind almonds if using whole ones 20s/sp6, put aside
3. Grind sugar 15s/sp10
4. Add orange peel, grind 20s/sp8
5. Add eggs, mix 2 min/sp4
6. Stir in almonds 5s/sp4

Non-Thermomix method

7. In food processor grind together almonds, sugar and zested peel
8. Add eggs and mix till smooth
9. Stir in ground almonds
10. Spread evenly in tin, bake 25-35 min
11. Sprinkle with icing sugar to serve

ORANGE/LEMON POLENTA CAKE GF

Number guests	6	12	18	24
Ground almonds (g)	100	200	300	400
Sugar (g)	100	200	300	400
Eggs	2	4	6	8
Butter (g)	100	200	300	400
Polenta (g)	50	100	150	200
Baking powder (tsp)	.5	1	1.5	2
Orange or orange peel	1	2	3	4
Syrup				
Orange or lemon juice	1	2	3	4
Icing sugar (g)	50	100	150	200

1. Oven 160, line cake tin

Thermomix method

2. Grind sugar and fruit peel 20s/Sp8
3. Add all other ingredients and mix 20-30s/sp6

Non-Thermomix method

4. Zest orange and then mix into all other ingredients
5. Bake 35-50 mins till knife comes out clean
6. While cake cooking boil together juice and sugar until the sugar is dissolved
7. When cake is cooked, prick the top with a fork and pour the warm syrup all over

DF – use Non-dairy spread

FREE FROM PASTRY

Number guests	6	12	18	24
Melted Butter or Non-dairy spread (g)	100	200	300	400
Eggs	2	4	6	8
Coconut flour (g)	75	150	225	300

1. Oven 180
2. Thermomix method
3. Warm butter 4min/50/sp5
4. Add eggs, coconut flour and pinch salt mix 10s/2
5. Scrape down and then mix again 30s/sp2
6. Non-Thermomix method
7. Warm butter in microwave
8. Mix in other ingredients until smooth
9. Roll out pastry between 2 sheets of baking paper and then transfer to baking dish
10. Remove top paper and blind bake for 15 mins

To make sweet pastry add sugar to taste

4 CHILDREN'S OPTIONS

Different companies, different rules and different parents' different requirements. Catering for children is tricky!

At one end of the spectrum, some companies arrange an earlier setting for children, simplifying the meal and offering a more 'child-friendly' option. At the other end of the spectrum, children eat with the adults and get what's on the menu. You are in a tricky position as you want happy guests but you also shouldn't be expected to drastically increase your cooking time and budget at short notice. If it's just a one off you probably will choose to just get on with whatever helps the parents. If you have many weeks with families check what your chalet owner/company expects you to offer.

Parents of fussy children usually cope if there is plenty of bread and fruit around. Not the healthiest of diets but for a week a bread stuffed child is probably a lot nicer to have around than a snivelling hungry one. I speak from experience as my eldest was a nightmare to feed. I felt it was my responsibility and not the chalet hosts to keep him from starving but welcomed a tolerant approach. It's hard enough as a parent feeling guilty that you are feeding a 'rubbish' diet to your own child when all the health messages scream '5 A Day' at you but if you are facing criticism from other people too it can ruin your holiday. My story ends well as he now eats everything and appears very healthy.

Don't scare children by giving them huge portions, they may well feel overwhelmed and eat less as a consequence. Much better to have child-friendly portions and the option for a top up for those who would like to. It's also great to have a few vegetable sticks or cheese sticks on the table as these are regarded as 'healthy' by parents. Many of your desserts may be too rich or have alcohol in so tweak accordingly. Don't add the Cointreau to the chocolate mousse until you have portioned off enough for the children. Rather than offering ice-cream as a backup put some chopped fruit portions on the table for those who don't select the dessert on offer.

Children rarely want three courses and in fact may have paid a reduced rate so are only expecting two. If you can serve a 'gentler' version of whatever the main meal is you'll be saving yourself loads of work, if not here are some child-friendly suggestions.

CHEESE AND HAM POTATO BAKE

Number guests	6	12	18	24
Potatoes thinly sliced(kg)	1	2	3	4
Sweetcorn (g)	150	300	450	600
Ham chopped (g)	150	300	450	600
Onion chopped	1	2	3	4
Butter (g)	50	100	150	200
Flour (g)	50	100	150	200
Milk (g)	500	1000	1500	2000
Grated cheese (g)	150	300	450	600
Parmesan grated (g)	50	100	150	200
Breadcrumbs (g)	50	100	150	200

1. Oven 180
2. Cook potatoes in boiling water for 5 mins, drain

Thermomix method white sauce

3. Cook butter, flour, milk and cheese 9 min/90/sp3, season

Saucepan method white sauce

4. Melt butter and stir in flour
5. Add milk and stir whilst sauce thickens
6. Stir in cheese until melted
7. In oven tray mix potatoes, ham, sweetcorn and onion
8. Cover with cheese sauce
9. Mix parmesan and breadcrumbs and spread over the top
10. Bake 30-45 mins until golden

Replace ham with tuna or cooked chicken

GF Use cornflour instead of plain flour, use GF bread to make breadcrumbs

DF Use soya milk, leave out cheese from sauce and don't add parmesan to breadcrumb mix

JACKETS

Number guests	6	12	18	24
Jacket potato	6	12	18	24

Clean and bake for approx. 1 hour @180

Offer children a selection of tuna, grated cheese, chopped ham etc

CREAMY CHICKEN AND LEEKS

Number guests	6	12	18	24
Chicken sliced	6	12	18	24
Butter (g)	50	100	150	200
Leeks chopped	6	12	18	24
Ham chopped (g)	150	300	450	600
Onion chopped	1	2	3	4
Flour (g)	30	60	90	120
Stock (kg)	1	2	3	4

1. Fry sliced chicken in butter until golden
2. Add leeks and cook for further 10 mins
3. Stir in flour and gradually add in stock whilst stirring
4. When sauce has thickened check seasoning
5. Serve with rice and peas

Replace chicken with cooked ham and don't fry to start with, just add to fried leeks

GF   Use cornflour instead of plain flour

DF   Replace butter with olive oil

CHICKEN STIR FRY

Number guests	6	12	18	24
Chicken sliced	6	12	18	24
Garlic chopped	3	6	9	12
Red Pepper sliced	3	6	9	12
Courgette in ribbons	3	6	9	12
oil (g)	30	60	90	120
Soy Sauce(g)	60	120	180	240
stock (g)	500	1000	1500	2000
Egg noodles (g)	300	600	900	1200

1. Fry garlic and chicken till chicken is golden
2. Add peppers and cook 5 minutes
3. Stir in courgette ribbons, soy sauce and stock, cook for further few minutes until chicken cooked through.
4. Cook noodles in boiling seasoned water until soft
5. Add cooked noodles to chicken and veg and stir

GF   Leave out egg noodles and serve with rice

BAKED CHICKEN OR FISH GOUJONS

Number guests	6	12	18	24
Chicken breast in strips	6	12	18	24
Fish in strips (g)	600	1200	1800	2400
Fresh Breadcrumbs (g)	200	400	600	800
Flour (g)	100	200	300	400
Eggs lightly beaten	5	10	15	20
Oil (g)	30	60	90	120

1. Oven 180
2. Season breadcrumbs in a bowl
3. Place flour in a separate bowl and eggs in a third bowl
4. Dip chicken OR fish in flour, then egg and then breadcrumbs
5. Lay bread-crumbed chicken on oiled tray and drizzle remaining oil over goujons
6. Bake for 25-30 mins turning mid cook time

GF Use GF breadcrumbs or a mixture of grated parmesan and ground almonds

TUNA, BROCCOLI AND PASTA BAKE

Number guests	6	12	18	24
Tuna (g)	400	800	1200	1600
Tinned tomatoes (kg)	1	2	3	4
Dried pasta shapes (g)	500	1000	1500	2000
Broccoli (g)	500	1000	1500	2000
Mascarpone (g)	300	600	900	1200
Grated cheese (g)	150	300	450	600
Breadcrumbs (g)	50	100	150	200

1. Oven 200
2. Cook pasta and add broccoli for last 3 mins cooking time
3. Mix together grated cheese and breadcrumbs
4. Warm tomatoes in saucepan and then stir in mascarpone
5. Add drained pasta and broccoli and drained tuna, season
6. Tip into oven proof dish, cover with cheese/breadcrumb mix
7. Cook in oven till golden approx. 10 min

GF Use GF pasta

DINNER

This book is not about gourmet. Instead, it is about home-cooked satisfying filling food. After a great day on the mountain, guests want to enjoy a relaxed tasty evening meal. With a little bit of effort, you can elevate your food so that the guests appreciate that they have hit lucky with you being their hosts. A swirl of cream and a few chopped herbs can transform a hearty bowl of soup to an elegant dish. A little heart of shortbread with a cream dessert finishes it off with a bit of style.

One of the things I found most daunting my first season was quantities. I dreaded serving as I was really scared we wouldn't have enough to go around, yet I didn't want to waste food and I also had my budget to bear in mind. A little thing that helped me was always having exactly the right number of plates ready to serve onto. For hot courses, ideally these plates will also be warm – makes all the difference as tepid food can be very off putting.

So how are you going to serve the food, do you plate it all up, plate part and let the guests add their own veg etc or do the guests help themselves to everything. Your company may have guidelines that they would like you to follow or you may be constrained by lack of large table serving dishes. There are pros and cons to these three options. Plating everything up is time consuming and leads to food waste as not everyone likes everything you have piled up. The guests helping themselves to everything is a bit of a free for all and you have no control on portion sizes. Sometimes the guests' tables are too small to put the accompaniments on so if there is no other table at the side to put the veg etc on you have little choice but to serve everything. In this case, you need to be extremely organised to serve up quickly and neatly otherwise those served first who choose not to start until everyone is served may have a long wait and then a chilly meal. It is a good idea to spread the plates out and serve up several at a time e.g. all meat on plates, then sides etc rather than complete each plate individually – that just takes tooooooooooo long.

You have gone to a lot of effort to produce a lovely meal so don't let your table, crockery and cutlery and spoil it. A mucky tablecloth is a bit off putting, more so a bit of something stuck to the corner of the plate or smeary cutlery. It doesn't take much longer to polish your cutlery as you lay up and that way you are also really paying attention as to whether it is properly clean.

5 SOUPS AND STARTERS

Soups and skiing go together well. A rich, delicious bowl of soup is really comforting and filling. I believe that you can serve soup every other day. Make sure you don't overlap the same vegetables as are the basis of the soup – e.g. carrot and coriander soup followed by zesty carrots with the main – oh yes and not carrot cake for that afternoon tea.

Soups are also excellent as you can make them in the morning whilst cooking breakfast and then you have less to do when you get in later. The same can be said for cold starters. If you are doing a hot starter try and put it on the menu for a day when the main can be prepped in the morning, otherwise you have a lot to do all at once. If your starters are vegetarian then you don't have to also make a vegetarian option. I'm going to suggests three basic types of starter, each with variations, pates, bruschetta/crostini and quiche/tarts and of course a backup super speedy starter for emergencies.

SPINACH SOUP

Number guests	6	12	18	24
Onion	1	2	3	4
Butter (g)	30	60	90	120
Flour (g)	30	60	90	120
Frozen spinach (g)	200	400	600	800
Stock (g)	250	500	750	1000
Milk (g)	500	1000	1500	2000
Nutmeg (tsp)	.5	1	1.5	2

Thermomix method (can make 12 portions at a time)
1. Chop onion and butter 5s/sp5
2. Add spinach and chop 15s/sp5
3. Sauté 5min/100/sp1
4. Add flour, stock, milk and seasoning Mix 10s/7
5. Cook 15min/100/sp2
6. Check Seasoning
7. Puree 1min/sp10

Non-Thermomix method
8. Chop onion and fry in butter
9. Add spinach, stir and sauté for 5min
10. Add flour, stock, milk and seasoning and mix
11. Cook 15 min stirring occasionally
12. Check Seasoning
13. Puree
14. **Serve with swirl of cream and dusting of nutmeg**

GF   Use cornflour

DF   Use soya milk and replace butter with olive oil

BUTTERNUT SQUASH/PUMPKIN

Number guests	6	12	18	24
Onion (g)	2	4	6	8
Olive oil (g)	40	80	120	160
Butternut squash (g)	1000	2000	3000	4000
Chilli	1	2	3	4
Stock (g)	750	1500	2250	3000

Thermomix Method
1. Chop onion, squash, chilli and oil 10 s/sp5
2. Sauté 5min/100/sp1
3. Add stock and seasoning
4. Cook 15min/100/sp2
5. Puree 1 min/sp9

Non-Thermomix method
6. Chop onion, squash, chilli
7. Sauté in oil
8. Add stock and seasoning
9. Cook until pumpkin is soft
10. Puree

Check seasoning and serve with sprinkled chopped herbs

VEGETABLE SOUP – use up left over vegetables

Number guests	6	12	18	24
Onion	1	2	3	4
Olive oil (g)	30	60	90	120
Garlic	1	2	3	4
Lentils (g)	50	100	150	200
Cooked Vegetables (g)	500	1000	1500	2000
Stock (g)	1000	2000	3000	4000

1. Chop onions, garlic and oil 5s/sp5 or chop by hand
2. Sauté 5min/100/sp1 or Sauté in saucepan
3. Add remaining ingredients, cook 15min/sp2 or in saucepan till soft
4. Puree 1min/sp9 or puree

These two soups are GF and DF

ALL IN ONE MUSHROOM SOUP

Number guests	6	12	18	24
Onion	2	4	6	8
Butter (g)	75	150	225	300
Corn Flour (g)	50	100	150	200
Mushrooms (g)	750	1500	2250	3000
Stock (g)	750	1500	2250	3000
Lemon juice (g)	30	60	90	120
Fresh Chopped parsley (g)	15	30	45	60
Cream	75	150	225	300

1. Thinly slice half the mushrooms and put aside
2. Add unsliced mushrooms, butter, cornflour, lemon juice, stock and parsley to a saucepan or Thermomix
3. Stir and cook for 10 minutes or 8min/100/sp3
4. Puree and season in Thermomix 30s/sp8
5. Add cream and sliced mushrooms and cook for 5 minutes or in Thermomix 5 min/90/sp 3
6. Serve with a swirl of cream and sprinkling of chopped parsley

DF   Use soya milk instead of cream and olive oil instead of butter

CREAMY ZUCCHINI SOUP

Number guests	6	12	18	24
Onion chopped	2	4	6	8
Garlic chopped	2	4	6	8
Stock (g)	750	1500	2250	3000
Courgettes(g) chopped	750	1500	2250	3000
Salt tsp	1	2	3	4
Pepper tsp	1/4	1/2	3/4	1
Butter (g)	15	30	45	60
Cream cheese or Laughing Cow (g)	60	120	180	240

1. Place all ingredients apart from butter and cream cheese in saucepan or Thermomix and cook for 15 minutes or 15min/100/sp 1
2. Add butter and cream cheese
3. Puree 1min/sp 8
4. Check seasoning
5. Serve with a sprinkle of fresh/dried oregano

DF   Use soya milk instead of cream and olive oil instead of butter

SPICED LENTIL AND TOMATO SOUP

Number guests	6	12	18	24
Onion chopped	3	6	9	12
Garlic chopped	2	4	6	8
Olive oil (g)	50	100	150	200
Stock (g)	500	1000	2000	3000
Tinned chopped tomatoes (g)	500	1000	2000	3000
Lentils (g)	150	300	450	600
Ground ginger (tsp)	1.5	3	4.5	6
Ground coriander (tsp)	1.5	3	4.5	6
Ground cumin (tsp)	1.5	3	4.5	6
Sweet paprika (tsp)	1.5	3	4.5	6
Pepper (tsp)	.5	1	1.5	2
Ground cinnamon (tsp)	1	2	3	4
Ground turmeric (tsp)	1	2	3	4
Chilli powder (tsp)	.5	1	1.5	2
Ground nutmeg (tsp)	.5	1	1.5	2
Salt (tsp)	1	2	3	4
Spice mix (tablespoon)	3	6	9	12

1. Sauté onions and garlic in olive oil for 5 minutes
2. Add all spices and stir for 1 minute
3. Add stock, tomatoes and lentils and cook for 15-25 minutes until lentils are tender
4. Check seasoning, add more spice mix or salt if necessary
5. Serve with fresh coriander leaves to decorate

To save loads of time mix up a jar of spice mix, as below

Use a yogurt pot for a measure, mix well and store in airtight jar

	cup
Ground ginger	3
Ground coriander	3
Ground cumin	3
Sweet paprika	3
Pepper	1
Ground cinnamon	2
Ground turmeric	2
Chilli powder	1
Ground nutmeg	1
Salt	2

This soup is GF and DF

MUSHROOM PATE

Number guests	6	12	18	24
Mushrooms (g) chopped	250	500	750	1000
Butter (g)	30	60	90	120
Garlic chopped	3	6	9	12
Cream cheese (g)	250	500	750	1000
Seasoning				

Thermomix method
1. **Sauté mushrooms**, garlic and butter 5min/100/sp2
2. **Pure**e 10s/sp8
3. **Add** cream cheese and seasoning, **puree** 20s/sp8

Non-Thermomix method
4. **Sauté** mushrooms, garlic and butter until soft
5. **Blitz** till smooth
6. **Add** cream cheese and seasoning and **blitz** till smooth

Serve on fresh salad

DF   Use non-dairy spread

LEMON TUNA PATE

Number guests	6	12	18	24
Tuna (g)	250	500	750	1000
Butter (g)	250	500	750	1000
Lemons – cut in half longways	3	6	9	12
Seasoning				

1. Juice the lemons and then set aside squeezed out lemon halves
2. In food processor or Thermomix mix tuna, lemon juice, butter and seasoning until smooth
3. Serve in lemon halves on a few salad leaves and ideally with something like melba toast

DF   Use non-dairy spread

Melba toast a great way to use up stale bread, see recipe later

HERBY CREAM CHEESE BALLS

Number guests	6	12	18	24
Firm Cream cheese (g)	300	600	900	1200
Chopped fresh herbs (g)	50	100	150	200
Cornflour (g)	30	60	90	120

1. Cover hands in cornflour and make small balls
2. Roll balls in chopped herbs
3. Serve on salad leaves with red pepper jam (see recipe in Vegetables, sides and sauces section).

Recipe is GF

CHRISTMAS OR SPECIAL OCCASION SMOKED SALMON PATE

Number guests	6	12	18	24
Leeks in 1 cm pieces (g)	50	100	150	200
Smoked salmon (g)	200	400	600	800
Cream cheese (g)	50	100	150	200
Double cream (g)	50	100	150	200
Lemon juice (g)	20	40	60	80
Black pepper to taste				

Thermomix method
1. Mix leeks, smoked salmon and cream cheese 10s/sp5
2. Add cream and lemon juice, mix 15s/sp5

Non-Thermomix method
3. In Food processor mix leeks, smoked salmon and cream cheese
4. Add cream and lemon juice and mix again
5. Add pepper to taste

Recipe is GF

MELBA TOAST

Number guests	6	12	18	24
Slices of bread depends on size	6-12	12-24	18-36	24-48

1. Oven 180
2. Remove crusts, cut through bread to make two very thin slices
3. Bake in oven until dry and crisp, store in an airproof container

Great way to use up spare bread, keeps well and a great garnish

WILD MUSHROOM TARTS

Number guests	6	12	18	24
Puff Pastry (g)	500	1000	1500	2000
Mushrooms sliced (g)	400	800	1200	1600
Garlic, chopped	1	2	3	4
Parsley chopped (g)	5	10	15	20
Butter (g)	50	100	150	200
Parmesan (g)	50	100	150	200

1. Oven 200, lightly oiled trays
2. Roll pastry and line trays, prick pastry and part bake 10 mins, remove from oven
3. Fry butter, mushrooms, garlic and parsley until no liquid left
4. Put mushroom mix in part cooked pastry cases, sprinkle Parmesan over the top
5. Bake 10-20 min

Anything from sliced courgettes to aubergines to peppers, either on their own or in combination.

DF   fry mushrooms in olive oil and leave off Parmesan

GOATS CHEESE, WALNUT AND SUNDRIED TOMATOES

Number guests	6	12	18	24
Puff Pastry (g)	500	1000	1500	2000
Goats cheese (g)	150	300	450	600
Pitted dates chopped	4	8	12	16
walnuts (g)	20	40	60	80
Sundried tomatoes (g)	150	300	450	600
Olive oil (g)	20	40	60	80

1. Oven 200, lightly oiled trays
2. Roll pastry and line trays, prick pastry and part bake 10 mins, remove from oven
3. Chop sundried tomatoes 5s/sp5 and spread over pastry
4. Mix together goat's cheese and chopped dates 3s/sp4
5. Spread goats cheese and dates over pastry and sprinkle with walnuts
6. Oven 180
7. Drizzle with oil and bake 15-25 min

Replace goats cheese with brie or camembert.

Replace walnuts with sliced pear

BAKED CAMEMBERT

Number guests	6	12	18	24
Camembert round in box	2	4	6	8
Garlic clove in halves	2	4	6	8
Rosemary sprig	1	2	3	4
Olive oil	5	10	15	20

1. Oven 180
2. Poke garlic halves and rosemary leaves into camembert, drizzle with oil
3. Bake 15-20 mins until soft and gooey
4. Serve with hunks of bread

BRIE EN CROUTE

Number guests	6	12	18	24
Puff Pastry (g)	500	1000	1500	2000
Brie (g)	300-400	600-800	900-1200	1200-1600
Butter (g)	15	30	45	60
Walnuts or pecans (g)	50	100	150	300
Cinnamon (tsp)	.5	1	1.5	2
Brown sugar (g)	25	50	75	100
Egg for glazing	1	1	2	2

1. Oven 200
2. Melt butter and sauté nuts until lightly coloured
3. Add cinnamon and stir, let nut mix cool
4. Roll out pastry
5. Place brie in centre of pastry, top with cooled nut mix and sprinkle with brown sugar
6. Gather up pastry and seal in the brie
7. Glaze with beaten egg
8. Bake 15-20 minutes until golden brown
9. Serve with hunks of bread

Replace nut mix with cranberry sauce or red onion marmalade (recipe in Vegetables, sides and sauces section)

BRUSCHETTA

Bruschetta is a great way of using up excess bread. There are endless toppings you could use.

Number guests	6	12	18	24
Base				
Sliced bread or large bread - I slice per guest, small loaf -2 slices	6/12	12/24	18/36	24/48
Garlic clove in halves	1	2	3	4
Olive oil (g)	30	60	90	120

1. Lightly toast the sliced bread
2. Rub toasted surface with a clove of garlic and drizzle on some olive oil
3. Add topping of your choice and grill if needed

Number guests	6	12	18	24
Toppings				
Mozzarella and tomatoes				
Mozzarella (g)	350	700	1050	1400
Cherry tomatoes (g), halved	500	1000	1500	2000
Fresh basil leaves (g)	10	20	30	40
Broccoli, mushrooms and feta				
Broccoli (g)	300	600	900	1200
Mushrooms (g) sliced	150	300	450	600
Feta (g)	300	600	900	1200
Garlic	2	4	6	8
Butter (g)	15	30	45	60
Pea Pesto				
Frozen peas (g)	400	800	1200	1600
Garlic	2	4	6	8
Parmesan (g) grated	75	150	225	300
Cherry tomatoes	250	500	750	1000

Mozzarella and tomatoes
1. Mix mozzarella, tomatoes, seasoning and a drizzle of olive oil.
2. Place mix on cooked base and cook in over 5-10 mins 180 until cheese has melted and turned golden
3. Sprinkle with chopped basil leaves and drizzle of olive oil to serve

Broccoli, mushrooms and feta
4. Cook broccoli in boiling water till just tender
5. Sauté mushrooms and garlic in butter 3 mins. Add cooked broccoli and season
6. Place broccoli and mushrooms on cooked base and top with crumbled feta
7. Place under grill for a couple of minutes until feta starts to soften, serve with a drizzle of olive oil

Pea Pesto
8. In food processor or Thermomix mix together peas, garlic, Parmesan and seasoning
9. Spread on cooked base and decorate with cherry tomato halves

6 MAINS

As a company, we generally don't put dishes on the menu that the guests will find in the mountain restaurants. Why, because the locals will do them better. There are a couple of exceptions, lasagne and Tartiflette, these are both such handy and straightforward recipes, I felt I needed to include them. We've had guest feedback requesting more local dishes but in the end, we have to do what we can do best and specific local food that is not! However, we try to use locally sourced ingredients and try to reflect something of the local region. We are aware of preferred herbs and can use these in our recipes to produce a more local, less British flavour.

This is a very personal thought of mine but I have an issue with roasts on the menu. Firstly, you've got to be good to make it all happen for big numbers at the same time, secondly because roasts are boringly British and many people abroad don't want such a stark reminder of home and thirdly because they are just so unimaginative.

TARTIFLETTE

Number guests	6	12	18	24
Potatoes (kg)	1.5	3	4.5	6
Large onion chopped	3	6	9	12
Olive oil (g)	30	60	90	120
Lardons (g)	200	400	600	800
Reblochon cheese in cubes (g)	300	600	900	1200
Double cream (g)	200	400	600	800

1. Boil thickly sliced (1.5cm) peeled potatoes in salted water 6-8 mins until just tender, drain DON'T OVERCOOK
2. While potatoes are cooking Sauté onion 5 mins
3. Add lardons and cook another 5-10 mins till onion golden
4. Remove onion and lardons from pan leaving as much fat in pan as possible
5. Brown cooked potato slices in pan
6. Assemble Tartiflette in oven dish – potatoes, lardons and onions and chunks of cheese
7. Pour cream over the top and season
8. Cook under grill for 5 mins

Serve hot from the oven with salad, cornichons (gherkins), pickled onions, charcuterie and crusty bread.

This recipe is GF

LASAGNA

Number guests	6	12	18	24
Mince (g)	400	800	1200	1600
Chopped onions (g)	3	6	9	12
Optional –lardons or pancetta (g)	100	200	300	400
Garlic	3	6	9	12
Olive oil (g)	30	60	90	120
Tomato puree (g)	50	100	150	200
Tinned tomatoes (g)	400	800	1200	1600
Red wine (g)	100	200	300	400
LASAGNE(g)	400	800	1200	1600
White sauce				
Parmesan cubed (g)	100	200	300	400
Butter (g)	100	200	300	400
Flour (g)	100	200	300	400
Milk (l)	1	2	3	4

1. In large saucepan cook onions and onions till golden
2. Stir in mince (and lardons/pancetta if using them), cook till browned
3. Add tomatoes, puree and wine, stir, season and simmer 30 mins
4. Grate parmesan 10s/sp 10 and set aside

Thermomix method

5. Make white sauce add milk, butter, flour and seasoning 10min/90/sp3

Non-Thermomix method

6. Melt butter, stir in flour and seasoning and cook for 3 minutes stirring. Stir in milk and continue cooking until sauce thickens
7. Place layer of lasagne at bottom of pan, cover with layer of meat sauce, top with white sauce
8. Repeat layers finishing with layer of lasagne with only white sauce on top
9. Sprinkle with Parmesan, bake in medium oven for 30-40 minutes until lasagne cooked.

Serve with green salad and a coleslaw

Chicken, sweetcorn and peppers with Mexican spices
Chilli con Carne lasagne
Chicken and creamy mushroom sauce

GF Use GF pasta sheets or slices of courgette that have been lightly fried in olive oil and use cornflour to thicken white sauce

DF Make white sauce from non-dairy spread and milk. Omit Parmesan

PUFF PASTRY PIES

BEEF AND BEER PIE

Number guests	6	12	18	24
Beef (cubes) (kg)	1	2	3	4
Seasoned flour (g)	30	60	90	120
Chopped onions (g)	3	6	9	12
Garlic	3	6	9	12
Butter (g)	100	200	300	400
Large Carrots in chunks	2	4	6	8
Button mushrooms (g)	200	400	600	800
Local beer (g)	400	800	1200	1600
Beef stock (g)	500	1000	150	2000
Thyme sprig	2	4	6	8
Puff Pastry (g)	400	800	1200	1600
Egg lightly beaten	1	2	3	4

1. Oven 220
2. Coat beef in seasoned flour and brown in half the butter
3. Add vegetables, herbs, stock and ale. Cover and simmer at least an hour till tender, longer is better
4. Put in large oven dish, cover with pastry, brush and seal with egg
5. Bake 20-30 mins until pastry is golden

CHICKEN AND MUSHROOM PIE

Number guests	6	12	18	24
Chicken(cubes) (kg)	1	2	3	4
Seasoned flour (g)	30	60	90	120
Chopped onions (g)	2	4	6	8
Butter (g)	100	200	300	400
Button mushrooms (g)	250	500	750	1000
Leeks (g) sliced	250	500	750	1000
Milk (g)	300	800	1200	1600
Chicken stock (g)	300	1000	150	2000
Thyme sprig	2	4	6	8
Puff Pastry (g)	400	800	1200	1600
Egg lightly beaten	1	2	3	4

1. Oven 220
2. Coat chicken in seasoned flour and brown in half the butter
3. Add vegetables, herbs, stock and milk. Cover and simmer till tender
4. Put in large oven dish, cover with pastry, brush and seal with egg
5. Bake 20-30 mins until pastry is golden

MINCE AND VEGETABLES PIE

This pie makes a good alternative to lasagne

Number guests	6	12	18	24
Mince (g)	750	1500	2250	3000
Chopped onions (g)	3	6	9	12
Garlic	1	2	3	4
Butter (g)	100	200	300	400
Large Carrots in chunks	2	4	6	8
Button mushrooms (g)	200	400	600	800
Leeks (g) sliced	200	400	600	800
Tin tomatoes (g)	400	800	1200	1600
Beef stock (g)	500	1000	150	2000
Oregano (g) chopped	5	10	15	20
Flour (g)	30	60	90	120
Puff Pastry (g)	400	800	1200	1600
Egg lightly beaten	1	2	3	4

1. In large saucepan cook onions and garlic in butter till golden
2. Stir in mince, cook till browned
3. Add flour and stir
4. Add tomatoes, vegetables, herbs and stock, stir, season and simmer at least 30 mins till reduced
5. Put in large oven dish, cover with pastry, brush and seal with egg
6. Bake 20-30 mins until pastry is golden

The pies work well with mashed potato or hasselbacks.

FOR ALL PIES

GF   Thicken filling with cornflour

Use a layer of thinly sliced sweet potatoes instead of pastry to top the pie

DF   Replace butter with olive oil

Replace milk with a Non-dairy milk for the chicken and mushroom pie

DUCK CASSOULET

Number guests	6	12	18	24
Confit duck legs	6	12	18	24
Shallots chopped	2	4	6	8
Garlic, chopped	2	4	6	8
Tinned tomatoes (g)	250	500	750	1000
Tinned white beans (g)	500	1000	1500	2000
Pancetta lardons (g)	300	600	900	1200
Garlic sausage (g)	300	600	900	1200
Chicken stock (ml)	200	400	600	800
Sprig rosemary chopped	1	2	3	4
Celery stick – chopped	1	2	3	4
Large carrot – cubed	1	2	3	4
Lemon juice (g)	10	20	30	40
Olive oil or duck fat(g)	30	60	90	120

1. Heat oil or duck fat and cook lardons 5 min
2. Add onion, garlic and cook 5 min
3. Add carrot and celery and cook 5 min
4. Add tomatoes and cook 10 mins
5. Add beans, sausage, stock, rosemary and lemon juice, cook gently for 1-2 hours
6. Crisp duck legs in hot oven and serve on cassoulet

Recipe is GF and DF

STICKY GINGER CHICKEN

Number guests	6	12	18	24
Chicken breast	6	12	18	24
Ginger (g)	20	40	60	80
Soy sauce (g)	20	40	60	80
Honey (g)	20	40	60	80
Lime	2	4	6	8
Garlic	2	4	6	8

1. Oven 200 and grease oven tray
2. Mix ginger, soy sauce, honey, lime juice and garlic 30s/sp7
3. Coat chicken in sauce and bake 20 – 25 mins

This recipe works well with a stir fry of vegetable

Use medallions of pork fillet instead of chicken

This recipe is GF and DF

ROASTED RED PEPPER, MOZZARELLA AND BASIL STUFFED CHICKEN

Number guests	6	12	18	24
Chicken breast	6	12	18	24
Frozen grilled peppers defrosted	2	4	6	8
Basil chopped	2	4	6	8
Mozzarella (g)	300	600	900	1200
Parmesan (g)	50	100	150	200
Oregano (g)	5	10	15	20

1. Oven 200
2. Butterfly chicken breasts, sprinkle with oregano, add layer red pepper, chopped basil and sliced Mozzarella
3. Close chicken and sprinkle top with more oregano
4. Bake 30 – 40mins
5. Put remaining Mozzarella on cooked chicken and sprinkle with grated Parmesan
6. Grill until cheese is brown and bubbly

This recipe is quite dry so needs a 'wet' potato recipe with it

Recipe is GF

DF   Replace Mozzarella with sliced mushrooms fried with garlic and don't top with Parmesan

PARMESAN CHICKEN

This is a super easy recipe and works well with Potatoes Boulangère and roasted vegetables

Number guests	6	12	18	24
Chicken breast	6	12	18	24
Butter (g)	100	200	300	400
Parmesan (g)	200	400	600	800

1. Oven 150
2. Melt butter
3. Line tray with greaseproof paper
4. Dip chicken in melted butter
5. Roll chicken in Parmesan
6. Bake 20 to 30 mins until chicken cooked through

Don't overcook the chicken it should be really moist

Recipe is GF

PORK FILLET MIGNON IN HONEY AND MUSTARD SAUCE

Number guests	6	12	18	24
Pork tenderloin (kg)	1	2	3	4
honey(g)	100	200	300	400
Cider vinegar (g)	50	20	30	40
Brown sugar (g)	30	60	90	120
Dijon mustard (g)	30	60	90	120

1. Oven 180
2. Mix together all sauce ingredients 15s/sp6
3. Coat pork and roast 20-30 mins basting a few times

Recipe is GF and DF

MEDITTERANEAN LAMB

Number guests	6	12	18	24
Lamb shanks	6	12	18	24
Chopped onions (g)	3	6	9	12
Olive oil (g)	30	60	90	120
Courgettes in chunks	3	6	9	12
Mixed peppers sliced	6	12	18	24
Garlic	3	6	9	12
Cherry tomatoes (g)	400	800	1200	1600
Ground cumin (g)	5	10	15	20
Ground coriander (g)	5	10	15	20
Paprika (g)	5	10	15	20
Stock (g)	250	500	750	1000

1. In large saucepan fry lamb and onion till golden
2. Add courgettes and continue to fry until courgettes begin to soften
3. Add peppers, spices and garlic continue to cook until peppers start to soften
4. Add stock, tomatoes and seasoning, stir and then simmer for between 15 and 20 mins until veg is tender.
5. Either remove lamb from shanks or serve whole with vegetables

ITALIAN BEEF CASSEROLE

Number guests	6	12	18	24
Beef in strips (g)	500	1000	1500	2000
Chopped onions (g)	3	6	9	12
Olive oil (g)	30	60	90	120
Mixed peppers sliced	2	4	6	8
Garlic	3	6	9	12
Tinned tomatoes (g)	500	1000	1500	2000
Sprig rosemary	1	2	3	4
Pitted olives (g)	100	200	300	400

1. In large saucepan soften onion and garlic in olive oil
2. Add beef strips, peppers, tomatoes and rosemary, bring to simmer and cook till beef is tender OR transfer to large oven pan, seal with foil and slow cook.
3. Top up with some stock if necessary.
4. When cooked stir in olives

Recipes are GF and DF

FISH PIE

Number guests	6	12	18	24
Fish (g)	750	1500	2250	3000
Milk (g)	600	1200	1800	2400
Butter (g)	100	200	300	400
Flour (g)	50	100	150	200
Cooked prawns (g)	150	300	450	600
Sweetcorn (g)	100	200	300	400
Courgettes (g) thinly sliced	1	2	3	4
Parsley (tbs) chopped	3	6	9	12
Topping				
Potatoes (kg) cooked	1	2	3	4
Butter (g)	50	100	150	200
Milk (g)	50	100	150	200
Cheese (g) grated	50	100	150	200

1. Oven 200
2. Lay fish in oven tray, season and pour over half the milk and a few dots of butter
3. Bake 15-20 mins
4. Pour off liquid and save
5. Remove fish skins and flake the cooked fish
6. In a saucepan, melt remaining butter, stir in flour, stir in saved fishy milk and add remaining milk, season and keep stirring until sauce thickens or in Thermomix butter, flour, two milks and seasoning 9 min/90/sp3
7. Puree cooked potatoes, butter and milk and seasoning till smooth
8. In oven-proof container mix fish, white sauce, prawns, sweetcorn, courgettes and parsley
9. Spread pureed potato over fish mix, make a pattern with a fork and sprinkle grated cheese to finish
10. Bake 30-40 mins until golden brown

Add different vegetables

Add chopped hard-boiled eggs

Top with puff pastry instead of potatoes

GF   Use cornflour

HERB CRUSTED SALMON

Number guests	6	12	18	24
Salmon steaks	6	12	18	24
Breadcrumbs (g)	75	150	225	300
Lemons - rind	3	6	9	12
Butter (g)	75	150	225	300
Chopped herbs - bunches	2	4	6	8

1. Line oven tray with greaseproof paper, oven 180
2. Blitz together breadcrumbs, lemon zest, butter and herbs
3. Cover salmon steaks with breadcrumb mix
4. Bake approx. 15 mins until cooked thru
5. Maybe sprinkle lemon juice on steaks when serving

Replace lemon with parmesan

Change combination of herbs

GF   use GF bread for breadcrumbs or ground almonds

DF   replace butter with olive oil

This is a great way of using up stale bread – dry the bread in low oven then blitz to breadcrumbs and store in an airtight container

Make up some flavoured oils to use as a garnish by adding chopped herbs or chillies

7 VEGETARIAN MAINS

It will save you time if you can find a similar style vegetarian main as the meat or fish one. This means that your side dishes will compliment both and you won't need to do extra dishes. Also, as you are thinking of things like the textures in the whole meal, the vegetarian will appreciate varied textures too, not soup followed by risotto followed by a runny dessert.

BAKED AUBERGINE MELTS

Number guests	6	12	18	24
Aubergines (double amount aubergines if you only have small ones)	3	6	9	12
Garlic finely sliced	1	2	3	4
Olive oil (g)	50	100	150	200
Oregano (g)	5	10	15	20
Tomatoes sliced	6	12	18	24
Mozzarella sliced (g)	200	400	600	800

1. Oven 180
2. Halve aubergines lengthways, sprinkle garlic and salt, drizzle with oil and bake 20-30 mins until soft
3. Arrange tomato slices and mozzarella on cooked aubergine and put back in oven for further 5 -10 mins until cheese has melted
4. Sprinkle with oregano to serve

Small whole aubergines look lovely if you cut them so as they can make a fan. Miss out baking until soft because you have thinner layers that need less cooking. Next place garlic, tomato slices and mozzarella between slices, drizzle with oil, bake and serve as above

ITALIAN STUFFED PEPPERS

Number guests	6	12	18	24
Peppers	6	12	18	24
Couscous (g)	250	500	750	1000
Boiling water (g)	400	800	1200	1600
Toasted Pinenuts (g)	50	100	150	200
Pitted olives (g)	50	100	150	200
Chopped feta (g)	100	200	300	400
Sun dried tomatoes (g)	100	200	300	400
Oregano and parsley (g)	10	20	30	40

1. Put couscous in boiling salted water and leave to stand for 10-15 mins
2. Drain excess water from couscous and stir in pinenuts, olives, feta, sun dried tomatoes and herbs
3. Stuff the peppers and bake for 15 – 25 mins

These are GF and DF

NUTTY RISSOLES

Number guests	6	12	18	24
Mixed nuts roughly chopped (g)	250	500	750	1000
Onions	1	2	3	4
Garlic finely sliced	1	2	3	4
Olive oil (g)	50	100	150	200
Dried mixed herbs (tsp)	2	4	6	8
Mushrooms chopped (g)	250	500	750	1000
Fresh breadcrumbs (g)	150	300	450	600
Tomato puree (g)	30	60	90	120
Parsley chopped (g)	5	10	15	20
Soy sauce (g)	5	10	15	20
Egg	1	2	3	4
Flour (g)	20	40	60	80

1. Fry onions and garlic till soft
2. Remove pan from heat and add all other ingredients apart from flour, stir till well mixed
3. Season
4. Roll heaped tablespoons on nut mix in flour and flatten into 7 cm rissoles
5. Leave in fridge for at least 1 hr
6. Fry in olive oil

This recipe is DF

GF   replace bread with GF bread and flour ground almonds

MUSHROOM PANCAKES

Number guests	6	12	18	24
Pancakes (see page 11)	12	24	36	48
Olive oil (g)	50	100	150	200
Wild mushrooms (g)	300	600	900	1200
Onion finely chopped	3	6	9	12
Garlic finely chopped	3	6	9	12
Dried mixed herbs (g)	5	10	15	20
Cream (g)	300	600	900	1200
Frozen spinach, defrosted, drained (g)	300	600	900	1200
Mozzarella sliced (g)	300	600	900	1200

1. Fry onions, garlic and mushrooms until lightly browned
2. Add herbs, cream and spinach, season and stir.
3. Make pancake parcels and top with slice of mozzarella
4. Melt cheese under grill

ROAST VEGETABLE CASSOULET

Number guests	6	12	18	24
Tinned white beans (kg)	1	2	3	4
Onions	3	6	9	12
Garlic finely sliced	3	6	9	12
Olive oil (g)	50	100	150	200
Thyme sprig, bay leaf, parsley, tarragon	1	2	3	4
Sugar (g)	5	10	15	20
Carrots (g)	500	1000	1500	2000
Celery sticks	3	6	9	12
Tinned tomatoes (g)	400	800	1200	1600
Butternut squash	1	2	3	4
Celeriac peeled	1	2	3	4
Dijon Mustard (g)	20	40	60	80
Parsley (g)	20	40	60	80
Bread (g)	100	200	300	400

1. Oven 200
2. Fry onions, celery and garlic until soft
3. Add tomatoes, sugar, herbs and beans, simmer 30 mins
4. Cut squash, celeriac and carrots into chunks and coat in oil
5. Roast veg for 30 mins
6. Add roasted veg, mustard and half the parsley into the beans
7. In Food processor blitz bread and parsley or in Thermomix turbo 4x2secs
8. Put bean and veg mix into oven tray, cover with parsley breadcrumbs, drizzle with oil and bake 40-50 mins until golden

This recipe is DF

GF   replace bread with GF bread

COURGETTES WITH GINGER AND GARLIC SAUCE

Number guests	6	12	18	24
Courgettes	12	24	36	48
Garlic finely chopped	3	6	9	12
Olive oil(g)	50	100	150	200
Chilli	1	2	3	4
Ginger finely chopped (g)	20	40	60	80
Onion	1	2	3	4
Soy sauce (g)	20	40	60	80
Vinegar (g)	20	40	60	80
Honey (tsp)	1	2	3	4

1. Oven 180
2. Halve courgettes lengthways, sprinkle with garlic and salt, drizzle with oil
3. Bake 15-20 mins until soft
4. In food processor or Thermomix blitz remaining oil, chilli, ginger, onion, soy sauce, vinegar and honey
5. Baste courgettes with marinade and bake further 5 mins

This recipe is GF and DF

WILD MUSHROOM TARTIFLETTE

Number guests	6	12	18	24
Potatoes, thickly sliced (kg)	1.5	3	4.5	6
Olive oil (g)	50	100	150	200
Wild mushrooms (g)	300	600	900	1200
Onion finely chopped	3	6	9	12
Garlic finely chopped	1	2	3	4
Dried mixed herbs (g)	5	10	15	20
Cream (g)	300	600	900	1200
Reblochon cheese in cubes(g)	300	600	900	1200

1. Soak dried mushrooms in water to rehydrate
2. Par boil potato slices until just tender
3. Fry onions, garlic and mushrooms until lightly browned
4. Brown cooked potato slices in pan
5. Assemble Tartiflette in oven dish – potatoes, mushrooms and onions and chunks of cheese
6. Pour cream over the top and season
7. Cook under grill for 5 mins

This recipe is GF

LENTIL AND VEGETABLE STEW

Number guests	6	12	18	24
Lentils (g)	400	800	1200	1600
Onions sliced	3	6	9	12
Garlic finely sliced	3	6	9	12
Olive oil (g)	50	100	150	200
Dried thyme	5	10	15	20
Peppers in slices	3	6	9	12
Celery sticks chopped	3	6	9	12
Tinned tomatoes (kg)	1	2	3	4
Courgettes chunked	3	6	9	12
Paprika (g)	5	10	15	20
Cumin (g)	5	10	15	20
Vegetable stock (g)	400	800	1200	1600

1. Fry onions, garlic, peppers and celery until soft
2. Add tomatoes, courgettes, herbs, spices, lentils and stock and simmer for 30 mins until lentils are cooked

Use different types of lentils
Replace courgettes with sliced carrots

This recipe is GF and DF

SPINACH AND MUSHROOM LASAGNA

Number guests	6	12	18	24
Lasagne (g)	300	600	900	1200
Onions	3	6	9	12
Garlic finely sliced	3	6	9	12
Olive oil (g)	50	100	150	200
Mushrooms sliced (g)	300	600	900	1200
Spinach defrosted (g)	750	1500	2250	3000
Lemon juice (g)	20	40	60	80
Nutmeg (tsp)	1	2	3	4
Ricotta (g)	300	600	900	1200
Cooking cheese (g)	150	300	450	600
White sauce				
Butter (g)		100	200	300	400
Flour (g)	100	200	300	400
Milk (l)	1	2	3	4
Grated Parmesan (g)	100	200	300	400

1. Oven 180
2. Drain defrosted spinach
3. Fry onions till soft
4. Add mushrooms and garlic, fry 5 mins
5. Add spinach, lemon juice and seasonings, cook 5 mins
6. Grate cooking cheese and mix with ricotta
7. Make white sauce in Thermomix all ingredients 9min/90/speed 3 or slow way in saucepan (melt butter, stir in flour, stir in milk, stir constantly while cooking and thickening sauce)
8. Add Parmesan to white sauce
9. Assemble lasagne in greased oven tray,
10. 1/3 pasta, half cheese mix, half mushroom/spinach, repeat and finish with a layer of lasagne
11. Cover with white sauce and bake 20-30 mins until golden

Replace mushrooms with tomatoes

Replace spinach with courgettes (fry courgettes first to soften)

GF   Use GF pasta sheets or cooked slices of aubergine, replace flour with cornflour

VEGETABLE GRATIN

Number guests	6	12	18	24
Veg (kg)	1	2	3	4
Onions	3	6	9	12
Garlic finely sliced	3	6	9	12
Olive oil (g)	50	100	150	200
Bread (g)	100	200	300	400
Garlic	3	6	9	12
Parsley (g)	20	40	60	80
Parmesan cubed (g)	50	100	150	200
Butter (g)	100	200	300	400
Flour (g)	100	200	300	400
Milk (l)	1	2	3	4

1. Oven 180
2. Cook chopped veg until tender, drain and place in greased oven tray
3. In Food processor bread, garlic, parsley and Parmesan or in Thermomix Turbo 6x2sec
4. Make white sauce in Thermomix all ingredients 9min/90/speed 3 or slow way in a saucepan. Saucepan method - melt butter, stir in flour, stir in m ilk, stir constantly while cooking and thickening sauce
5. Cover cooked veg with white sauce and then breadcrumb topping to finish
6. Bake 15-20 mins till golden

CELEBRATION NUT ROAST

Number guests	6	12	18	24
Aubergine thinly sliced	2	4	6	8
Onions sliced	2	4	6	8
Garlic finely chopped (g)	2	4	6	8
Celery stick chopped	2	4	6	8
Olive oil (g)	50	100	150	200
Nuts roughly chopped (g)	300	600	900	1200
Lemon juice (g)	20	40	60	80
Breadcrumbs(g)	100	200	300	400
Cooking cheese (g)	100	200	300	400
Eggs	2	4	6	8
Parsley chopped (g)	20	40	60	80

1. Oven 180, grease loaf tin
2. Dip aubergines in oil, season and bake on tray until golden
3. Line aubergine slices in loaf tin, dangling ends of slices over the side
4. Fry onions, garlic and celery until soft and put into large bowl
5. Add remaining ingredients and mix well
6. Add nut mixture into aubergine lined tin. Push down and enclose with ends of aubergine
7. Cover with foil. Bake 45 min - hour

GF   Use GF bread

8 VEGETABLES, SIDES AND SAUCES

With a little extra effort, you can easily transform a straightforward meal to a memorable one. No one remembers a meat, potatoes and two over cooked plain vegetables main meal or if they do its probably for the wrong reasons. Potatoes, rice or pasta that set off the main, vegetables that have been garnished and a little bit of sauce, if appropriate will elevate the dinner to a much higher standard. It's important to not go over the top and throw so many extras on the plate that the star of the plate is lost. Think about what finishing you want to add to the vegetables to compliment the main, think about whether the plate needs crisp potatoes or would mash be just the thing. It's all about balance. Pre-season, make sure you've tried out your menu, get feedback, as much as you can and then use the comments to tweak your menu.

QUANTITIES OF VEGETABLES AND SERVING SUGGESTIONS

Number guests	6	12	18	24
Potatoes (kg)	1.5	3	4.5	6
Vegetables (g)	500	1000	1500	2000

WAYS OF TARTING UP VEGETABLES

Sprinkle with fresh chopped herbs

Number guests	6	12	18	24
Herbs (g)	5	10	15	20

Melted butter and lemon zest

Number guests	6	12	18	24
Butter melted (g)	50	100	150	200
Lemon (zest)	1	2	3	4

Sprinkle with freshly chopped nuts or sliced almonds

Number guests	6	12	18	24
Nuts (g)	50	100	150	200

Herb Butter

Number guests	6	12	18	24
Butter melted (g)	50	100	150	200
Herbs (g)	5	10	15	20

Blitz butter and herbs together in food processor or Thermomix

Crispy onions and seeds

Number guests	6	12	18	24
Onions cut into thin rings	1	2	3	4
Sunflower or pumpkin seeds (g)	30	60	90	120

Fry the onions till crispy

Contrasting colour peppers

Number guests	6	12	18	24
Peppers	1	2	3	4

Add thinly sliced peppers either raw or lightly fried to provide a bright colour contrast

CRISPY COURGETTES

Number guests	6	12	18	24	30	36	42	48	54	60
Courgettes (g)	50	100	150	200	250	300	350	400	450	500
Garlic	1	2	3	4	5	6	7	8	9	10
Seasoned flour	150	300	450	600	750	900	1050	1200	1350	1500

1. Put seasoned flour in plastic bag
2. Add courgettes and shake till they are lightly coated
3. Heat oil and cook garlic
4. Fry courgettes in batches and keep warm till ready to serve

POTATOES

Number guests	6	12	18	24
Potatoes (kg)	1.5	3	4.5	6

Dauphinoise

Number guests	6	12	18	24
Potatoes thinly sliced (kg)	1.5	3	4.5	6
Cream (g)	500	1000	1500	2000
Milk (g)	500	1000	1500	2000
Garlic	3	6	9	12

1. Oven 180
2. Bring milk, garlic and cream to the boil
3. Add potatoes, seasoning and simmer for 3-5 mins until potatoes nearly cooked
4. Pour cream and potatoes into oven tray and bake 30-45 min until potatoes soft and golden

Boulangère

Number guests	6	12	18	24
Potatoes thinly sliced (kg)	1.5	3	4.5	6
Onions thinly sliced	2	4	6	8
stock (g)	400	800	1200	1600
Parmesan grated (g)	50	100	150	200

1. Oven 180
2. In oven tray make layers of sliced potato, onion and seasoning. For final layer overlap the potatoes
3. Pour over stock and add more seasoning and sprinkle Parmesan over the top
4. Bake for approx. 1 hour until potatoes are soft and top layer is crisp and golden

Hasselback

Number guests	6	12	18	24
Potatoes thinly sliced (kg)	1.5	3	4.5	6
Rosemary sprigs chopped	2	4	6	8
Garlic finely chopped	2	4	6	8
Olive oil (g)	50	100	150	200

1. Oven 180
2. Cook potatoes in pan of boiling water for 5 mins, drain and cool
3. Insert skewer through potato and make cuts as deep as the skewer
4. Place potatoes in oven tray, sprinkle garlic and rosemary and season
5. Drizzle with olive oil and bake 30-45 mins until golden

SAUCES AND EXTRAS

RED PEPPER SAUCE

Number guests	6	12	18	24
Red peppers sliced	3	6	9	12
Olive oil (g)	30	60	90	120
Garlic	2	4	6	8
Onion	1	2	3	4
Stock (g)	150	300	450	600

1. Oven 200
2. Brush peppers with oil and bake till soft
3. In Food processor chop onions and garlic or in Thermomix 5s/sp5
4. Sauté in frying pan or in Thermomix 5min/100/sp2
5. Add peppers, stock, cook 10min stirring or in Thermomix 10mins/100/sp1
6. Puree sauce or in Thermomix 1min/sp9
7. If sauce is bitter add a little sugar and re blend for 15 seconds

BALSAMIC REDUCTION

Number guests	6	12	18	24
Balsamic vinegar (g)	500	1000	1500	2000
Honey or brown sugar (g)	60	120	180	240

1. In a saucepan cook vinegar and honey/sugar and cook 25 minutes stirring occasionally.
2. In Thermomix cook 25min/Varoma/sp 1 **Measuring Cap Off**
3. Test for consistency - dip spatula into reduction to coat. Run a fingertip across reduction, if it leaves a path the reduction is done, if not cook again in three-minute sessions and keep re-testing
4. Store in jar

Great for decorating plates and adding a bit of 'oomph' to things like goat's cheese tart

CARAMELIZED ONIONS

Number guests	6	12	18	24
Onion (g) in quarters	500	1000	1500	2000
Olive oil (g)	30	60	90	120
Garlic	2	4	6	8
Salt (g)	10	20	30	40
Soy sauce (g)	15	30	45	60
Vinegar (g)	25	50	75	100
Sugar (g)	50	100	150	200

Thermomix method
1. Put onion, garlic, salt and oil in Thermomix and chop 4s/sp5
2. Cook 8min/Varoma/REVERSE/ Sp 1
3. Add soy sauce, vinegar and sugar Mix 2s/REVERSE/sp2
4. Cook 15 min/100/REVERSE/Sp1 MEASURING CAP OFF

Non-Thermomix method
5. Chop onions and garlic and fry in olive oil with salt for 10 mins
6. Add remaining ingredients and cook for 15 mins stirring to stop mix sticking

Store in jar

RED PEPPER JAM

Number guests	6	12	18	24
Red peppers quarters (g)	600	1200	1800	2400
Sugar (g)	200	400	600	800
White wine vinegar (g)	100	200	300	400
Water (g)	50	100	150	200

Thermomix method
1. Chop peppers 5s/sp4
2. Scrape down, add remaining ingredients and Cook 35min/Varoma/spoon/REVERSE. Replace measuring cap with steaming basket
3. Non-Thermomix method
4. Chop peppers and place in saucepan
5. Add remaining ingredients and cook for between 30 and 40 mins, stirring until mixture has thickened

Store in jar

Great with a cheese platter or to accompany starters using cheese

PICANTE SAUCE

Number guests	6	12	18	24
Chilli (tsp)	1	2	3	4
Onion	1	2	3	4
Garlic	1	2	3	4
Olive oil (g)	20	40	60	80
Cinnamon (tsp)	1	2	3	4
Thyme (tsp)	1	2	3	4
Tinned tomatoes (g)	400	800	1200	1600
Vinegar (g)	20	40	60	80
Stock (g)	400	800	1200	1600

1. Fry onion and garlic till soft
2. Add all other ingredients and simmer 30 min – 45 min till reduced, check seasoning

Goes well with Nut Roast and Nutty Rissoles

9 SALADS

We introduced a salad option into some of our larger chalets a few years ago. Vegetarians and those with dietary requirements should have notified us in advance. Some guests really don't want the main and in the smaller chalets, that's tough as we don't have the budget to let pre-bought items go to waste. In the larger chalets, we go around after dinner and let people know what the main dish will be the next night. We also let them know the salad option and if they choose then, they can select the salad option. The more choices you offer, the higher will be your spend and sadly the more food will go to waste.

NICOISE SALAD

Number guests	6	12	18	24
Tuna (kg)	1	2	3	4
New Potatoes (kg)	1	2	3	4
Eggs hard boiled halved	12	24	36	48
Green beans (g)	300	600	900	1200
Crisp lettuce in wedges	3	6	9	12
Olive oil (g)	150	300	450	600
Cherry tomatoes (g)	600	1200	1800	2400
Balsamic vinegar (g)	30	60	90	120
Lemon juice (g)	50	100	150	200
Dressing	5	10	15	20
Black olives (g)	150	300	450	600
Anchovies (g)	50	100	150	200
Garlic	3	6	9	12
Lemon (g)	50	100	150	200
Olive oil (g)	250	500	750	1000
Balsamic vinegar (g)	30	60	90	120

1. Blitz dressing ingredients in food processor or Thermomix 20s/sp10
2. Cook potatoes 15-20 mins until tender, drain and cool in cold water
3. Cook beans 5 mins until tender, drain and cool in cold water
4. Halve potatoes and fry them till golden
5. Add tomatoes and fry 1 min, add vinegar and remove from heat
6. Mix lemon juice and oil and stir over lettuce wedges
7. Assemble salad and dollop spoonful of olive dressing on each egg half

CAESAR SALAD

Number guests	6	12	18	24
Ciabatta loaf in chunks	2	4	6	8
Olive oil (g)	100	200	300	400
Chicken breast	3	6	9	12
Lg Crispy lettuce in wedges	2	4	6	8
Garlic	2	4	6	8
Anchovies	10	20	30	40
Mayonnaise (g)	100	200	300	400
White wine vinegar (g)	20	40	60	80
Parmesan shavings (g)	10	20	30	40

1. Sprinkle olive oil and seasoning over bread chunks and bake 10 mins @180
1. Fry chicken breasts until cooked through
2. Blitz garlic, anchovies, mayonnaise, vinegar and seasoning in food processor or Thermomix, should be consistency of yoghurt, add water to thin if necessary
3. Assemble salad and sprinkle parmesan shavings on top to finish

GF   Use GF bread
DF   Leave off Parmesan shavings

FOUR SEASONS SALAD

Number guests	6	12	18	24
Prosciutto slices	12	24	36	48
Butter (g)	30	60	90	120
Sundried tomatoes (g)	30	60	90	120
Large Crispy lettuce in wedges	2	4	6	8
Mushrooms sliced (g)	100	200	300	400
Capers (g)	30	60	90	120
Mozzarella sliced (g)	100	200	300	400
White wine vinegar (g)	20	40	60	80
Mayonnaise (g)	100	200	300	400
Garlic	1	2	3	4

1. Fry mushrooms in butter and then allow to cool
2. Blitz garlic, mayonnaise, vinegar and seasoning in food processor or Thermomix, should be consistency of yogurt, add water to thin if necessary
3. Assemble salad

Vegetarian   Leave out Prosciutto and replace with olives
DF   Use olive oil and replace Mozzarella with Olives

GOAT'S CHEESE SALAD

Number guests	6	12	18	24
Red Onion finely chopped	1	2	3	4
Pancetta chopped (g)	100	200	300	400
Brown bread sliced	2	4	6	8
Goats cheese (g)	300	600	900	1200
Hazelnuts (g)	100	200	300	400
Mixed salad leaves (g)	600	1200	1800	2400
White wine vinegar (g)	30	60	90	12-
Olive oil (g)	150	300	450	600
Parsley chopped (g)	5	10	15	20
Thyme (g)	5	10	15	20
Lemon juice (g)	20	40	60	80

1. Fry pancetta till crisp
2. Blitz together onion, vinegar, olive oil, lemon juice and herbs in food processor or Thermomix 10s/sp10
3. Mix together leaves, fried pancetta, nuts and dressing
4. Toast bread, grill goat's cheese on top till golden and serve on top of salad

Vegetarian   Leave out Pancetta
GF   Use GF bread

GREEK SALAD

Number guests	6	12	18	24
Red Onion finely chopped	1	2	3	4
Tomatoes in wedges(kg)	3	6	9	12
Cucumber peeled and thickly sliced	1	2	3	4
Pepper cut into chunks	2	4	6	8
Olives (g)	100	200	300	400
Feta (g)	300	600	900	1200
Dried oregano (g)	5	10	15	20
Olive oil (g)	150	300	450	600

Combine all ingredients together and season

Make up large quantities of dressings and store in large bottles

10 DESSERTS

A good dessert sends your guests to bed with a smile on their faces. Ice-cream and fruit salad do not - boring. It is easier for you to have already prepped your dessert and have it ready to go after the main. Having a dessert that needs serving hot means good planning for oven use and not getting distracted when serving out the main so as to end up with a burnt offering. And just the same as with your starters and mains, a little thought to presentation and finish can elevate a humble chocolate mousse to a restaurant worthy pudding.

PAVLOVA

Number guests	6	12	18	24
Meringue				
Sugar (g) **approx.**	225	450	675	900
Egg whites	4	8	12	16
Topping				
Cream (g)- whipped	500	1000	1500	2000
Fruit (g)	750	1500	2250	3000

1. Oven 100, line trays with greaseproof paper
2. Weigh egg whites and note down weight, whisk egg whites till stiff in large bowl
3. Weigh **double** the weight of sugar to noted down egg white weight
4. Whilst whisking very slowly whisk in sugar until mixture is stiff
5. Pipe pavlova bases onto lined trays and dry out in oven for two hours
6. Assemble pavlovas with whipped cream and fruit

EMERGENCY DESSERT – FRUITS OF THE FOREST SYLLABUB

Number guests	6	12	18	24
Sugar (g)	150	300	450	600
Dessert wine (g)	200	400	600	800
Cream (g) - whipped	300	600	900	1200
Frozen berries (g)	300	600	900	1200

1. In Food Processor blend sugar with half the fruit or in Thermomix 20s/sp6, set aside,
2. Whisk cream or in Thermomix, Insert butterfly whisk and whip cream on speed 3.5 till stiff
3. In Food processor add and mix blended fruit and dessert wine, In Thermomix mix 20s/sp6
4. Gently stir in remaining fruit by hand
5. Serve in glasses

These two desserts are GF

CRÈME BRULEE

Number guests	6	12	18	24
Sugar (g)	40	80	120	160
Cream (g)	300	600	900	1200
Eggs	3	6	9	12
Vanilla essence(tsp)	1	2	3	4
Topping or finish				
Brown sugar (g)	150	300	450	600
Variation				
Frozen berries (g)	150	300	450	600

Thermomix method

1. Mix all ingredients apart from brown sugar 1min/Sp3
2. Cook 10min/90/sp3 OR for 14 mins if cream was cold to start (for 18 portions cook for 30min/90/speed 3
3. If cream doesn't thicken cook for 2 mins/90/sp3
4. If cream has gone grainy or scrambled add 30g cold milk and blend 30s/8, repeat if necessary.
5. Pour into ramekins and let cool to thicken.

Non-Thermomix method

6. Oven 150
7. Heat cream and vanilla in a saucepan until boiling and then simmer for 5 minutes
8. As cream is heating up, beat egg yolks and sugar together in a large bowl until lighter
9. Pour simmering cream over egg yolk mix whilst whisking and keep beating until mixture is thickened
10. Strain the mixture through a sieve and then pour into ramekins (2/3 full)
11. Place the ramekins in a deep oven tray and add water to come half way up ramekins
12. Cook for 40-45 minutes until set
13. Remove from waterbath and allow to cook

Cover with brown sugar and then either place under grill or use blow torch to caramelise the top

A QUICK DESSERT – In ramekins, pour hot crème brulee mix over frozen berries and serve immediately

This is a GF dessert

LEMON TART

Number guests	6	12	18	24
SWEET PASTRY				
Icing sugar (g)	100	200	300	400
Butter (g)	250	500	750	1000
Flour (g)	350	700	1050	1400
Egg yolks)	3	6	9	12
(Pre-made pastry shell if using)	1	2	3	4
FILLING				
Sugar (g)	75	150	225	300
Lemon peel from	3	6	9	12
Lemon juice (g)	75	150	225	300
Cream (g)	125	250	375	500
Eggs	4	8	12	16

1. Oven 180 and lightly grease patty tin
2. In Food processor or Thermomix Turbo butter, flour and icing sugar until mixture looks like breadcrumbs
3. Add egg yolks and mix few seconds, in Thermomix reverse/speed 3 until mixture JUST coming together
4. Tip pastry out, wrap in cling-film and place in fridge for an hour before rolling out (can freeze at this stage for later use)
5. Roll out and bind bake till golden

Filling Thermomix method
6. Grind sugar 5s/sp10
7. Add lemon peel and grind 20s/sp10
8. Scrape down and add lemon juice, cream and eggs. Cook 7 min/80/sp3
9. Taste, add more lemon or sugar if necessary
10. Cook 45s/90/sp5 and then pour immediately into cooled pastry shell and leave to set for at least 3 hours

Filling Non-Thermomix method
11. Zest lemons and then cook all ingredients in a saucepan, stirring continuously until the mixture has thickened.
12. Puree with food processor or stick blender then pour immediately into cooled pastry shell and leave to set for at least 3 hours

Replace lemon with orange

FRUIT TART – crème patisserie and fruit

Number guests	6	12	18	24
SWEET PASTRY				
Icing sugar (g)	100	200	300	400
Butter (g)	250	500	750	1000
Flour (g)	350	700	1050	1400
Egg yolks)	3	6	9	12
(Pre-made pastry shell if using)	1	2	3	4
Filling				
Milk (g)	250	500	750	1000
Sugar (g)	30	60	90	120
Cornflour (g)	20	40	60	80
Eggs	2	4	6	8
Egg yolks	2	4	6	8
Fruit (g)	250	500	750	1000
Jam (glaze) (g)	50	100	150	200

1. Oven 180 and lightly grease patty tin
2. In Food processor or Thermomix Turbo butter, flour and icing sugar until mixture looks like breadcrumbs
3. Add egg yolks and mix few seconds, in Thermomix reverse/speed 3 until mixture JUST coming together
4. Tip pastry out, wrap in cling-film and place in fridge for an hour before rolling out (can freeze at this stage for later use)
5. Roll out and bind, bake till golden
6. Cook milk, sugar, cornflour, eggs and egg yolks stirring constantly or in Thermomix 7min/90/sp4
7. Cool and spread over pastry
8. Cover with fruit
9. Heat jam and then glaze fruit to finish

CHOCOLATE ORANGE MOUSSE

Number guests	6	12	18	24	30	36	42	48	54	60
Dark chocolate g)	200	400	600	800	1000	1200	1400	1600	1800	2000
Sugar (g)	50	100	150	200	250	300	350	400	450	500
Orange peel	1	2	3	4	5	6	7	8	9	10
Eggs separated	4	8	12	16	20	24	28	32	36	40
Cream (g)	100	200	300	400	500	600	700	800	900	1000

1. Grind sugar and orange peel 15s /sp10 and scrape down sides
2. Add chocolate and cream and melt 4min/50/sp2
3. In large bowl whisk egg whites till stiff
4. Add egg yolks to chocolate mix and stir 15s/sp4
5. Gently fold in chocolate mix to stiff egg whites
6. Pour into glasses or ramekins and let set for 3-4 hours

SPEEDY CHOCOLATE SAUCE DESSERTS

CHOCOLATE SAUCE

Number guests	6	12	18	24
Dark chocolate (g)	250	500	750	1000
Butter (g)	40	80	120	160
Milk (g)	200	400	600	800

Melt chocolate, butter and milk in saucepan stirring continuously or in Thermomix 4-5mins/100/sp2

DAME BLANCHE/DAMA BIANCA (Hot fudge sundae)

Number guests	6	12	18	24
Vanilla ice-cream (l)	1	2	3	4
Cream (g)	150	300	450	600

1. Whip cream till stiff
2. Make chocolate sauce as above
3. Serve 3 scoops ice-cream with hot chocolate sauce and top with whipped cream

Increase the fat level in the cream to help it whip up by adding Mascarpone

CHOCOLATE PEARS

Number guests	6	12	18	24
Poached pears	6	12	18	24
Vanilla ice-cream (l)	.5	1	1.5	2

Pour hot chocolate sauce over poached pears and serve with large scoop of ice-cream

CARAMELIZED BANANAS IN CHOCOLATE SAUCE

Number guests	6	12	18	24
Brown sugar (g)	100	200	300	400
Butter (g)	50	100	150	200
Bananas, sliced length-wise	6	12	18	24
Vanilla ice-cream (l)	.5	1	1.5	2
OR Cream (g)	150	300	450	600

1. Heat butter in frying pan, add sliced bananas, sprinkle over sugar
2. Cook till bananas are soft
3. Serve bananas with hot chocolate sauce and either dollop of whipped cream or scoop of vanilla ice-cream

STICKY TOFFEE PUDDING AND SAUCE

Number guests	6	12	18	24
Pudding				
Pitted dates (g)	150	300	450	60
Bicarb (tsp)	1.5	3	4.5	6
Boiling Water (g)	180	360	540	720
Butter (g)	50	100	150	200
Dark sugar (g)	100	200	300	400
Plain flour (g)	150	300	450	600
Milk (g)	50	100	150	200
Baking powder (tsp)	.5	1	1.5	2
Egg	1	2	3	4
Sauce				
Butter (g)	50	100	150	200
Dark sugar (g)	50	100	150	200
Golden syrup (g)	75	150	225	300
Milk (g)	50	100	150	200
Vanilla essence (tsp)	1	2	3	4

1. Oven 180 Grease deep tray
2. Soak dates and bicarb in boiling water for 30 mins
3. In Food processor mix soaked dates, liquid and all other pudding ingredients till smooth or in Thermomix 20s/Sp5
4. Cook pudding in greased tray for 20-30 mins until top bounces back when pushed
5. While pudding cooking make sauce
6. Place all sauce ingredients in saucepan, cook whilst stirring or in Thermomix 7min/100/sp2
7. Portion up and pour sauce over the top to serve

GF   Use GF flour

PANNA COTTA

Number guests	6	12	18	24
Gelatine sheets	3	6	9	12
Icing Sugar (g)	50	100	150	200
Cream (g)	600	1200	1800	2400
Vanilla essence(tsp)	1	2	3	4

1. Soak gelatine sheets in cold water
2. Cook sugar, cream and vanilla in saucepan till boiling or in Thermomix 8min/100/sp 2
3. Whisk in soaked gelatine sheets or with TMX running on speed 4 drop drained gelatine sheets through hole in lid, mix 15 sec.
4. Pour into moulds or glasses
5. Serve with coulis or berries

TIRAMISU

Number guests	6	12	18	24
Mascarpone g)	500	1000	1500	2000
Sugar (g)	25	50	75	100
Eggs separated	6	12	18	24
Cold coffee (ml)	300	600	900	1200
Sponge fingers (packet)	1	2	3	4
Marsala/sweet wine (ml)	50	100	150	200
Cocoa to garnish				

1. Whisk egg whites till stiff in large bowl
2. Mix mascarpone, sugar and egg yolks in food processor or in Thermomix 15s/sp 5
3. GENTLY Combine egg mixes together in large bowl
4. Put cold coffee and sweet wine in bowl
5. Dip half the sponge fingers in coffee mix and lay next to one another in serving dish (there shouldn't be any gaps)
6. Cover coffee soaked fingers with half the egg mix
7. Repeat 5 and 6
8. Leave in cool place to set
9. Thickly sprinkle cocoa over all the surface and score with knife

I love this Tiramisu recipe given to me by a lovely lady at the checkout of the mini supermarket in the village in the Dolomites where I did my first season. Fast, easy and impresses every time.

FROZEN FRUIT SORBET – for Thermomix users, doubt a food processor is powerful enough

Number guests	6	12	18	24
Sugar(g)	75	150	225	300
Frozen fruit (g)	500	1000	1500	2000
Lemon juice (g)	20	40	60	80
Egg white	1	2	3	4

1. Grind sugar 10s/sp10
2. Add other ingredients and blend 1min30s/Sp5 using spatula to move fruit around
3. Insert butterfly whisk and whisk 1min/sp 3.5
4. Serve with berries

Great way to use up older fruit – chop, freeze on a tray and then bag and keep in freezer until needed. Some frozen banana gives sorbet a creamier texture

This recipe is GF and DF

FRUIT CRUMBLE

Number guests	6	12	18	24
Pudding				
Fruit (g) – chopped	600	1200	1800	2400
Sugar (g)- depends on sweetness of fruit	50-100	100-200	150-300	200-400
Spice (tsp) optional	1	2	3	4
Topping				
Butter (g) in cubes	100	200	300	400
Sugar (g) demerara is good in topping	100	200	300	400
Plain flour (g)	200	400	600	800

1. Oven 180
2. Soften fruit in saucepan with sugar, spice and a little water
3. Make crumble topping by blitzing topping ingredients in food processor or in Thermomix Turbo 2x1s
4. Put softened fruit into oven proof dish (check sweetness and add more sugar if necessary)
5. Spread topping mix over fruit and bake for 20-30 mins until golden
6. Serve with custard, recipe below, ice cream or cream

All sorts of fruit combinations

Add some sliced almonds to the finished topping mix if no guests have nut allergies

DF Use dairy free spread in topping
GF Use GF flour in topping or make up own 'flour' using 2 Rice flour:1 Oats:1 sliced almonds

Excellent way of using up excess fruit

CUSTARD

Number guests	6	12	18	24
Milk (g)	500	1000	1500	2000
Vanilla essence (g)	5	10	15	20
Eggs	2	4	6	8
Sugar (g)	50	100	150	200
Cornflour (tbs)	2	4	6	8

Thermomix method
1. Mix all ingredients 10s/sp5 then cook 7min/90/sp3

Non-Thermomix method
2. In saucepan heat milk.
3. Whisk together vanilla essence, eggs, sugar and cornflour. Add hot milk continually whisking
4. Transfer back to the sauce pan stirring continually until custard thickens

DF   Use non-dairy milk

FRUIT TRIFLE

A bit retro but quick easy and a great emergency pudding

Number guests	6	12	18	24
Cake (g)	100-150	200-300	300-450	400-600
Fruit (g)	250	500	750	1000
Sherry or sweet wine	50	100	150	200
Custard – recipe above for	6	12	18	24
Cream (g) whipped	300	600	900	1200
Sliced toasted almonds (g)	50	100	150	200

1. Crumble cake into large bowl or individual serving dishes
2. Drizzle with sherry and stir in fruit
3. Cover with layer of thick custard
4. Top with whipped cream
5. Decorate with toasted almonds

Great way to use up stale cake

FINAL WORDS

I can't say it enough: be organized, look after your guests and make sure they have a holiday they remember for all the right reasons.

Start as you mean to go on and don't worry if things seem to be taking a little longer than you expected, you will speed up once you are familiar with your menu and daily routine. Christmas and New Year will slow you down a little because just when you were hitting your stride the menu changes and often there are more children around!

Sometimes chalet hosts hit the January blues, usually because they have become over-tired after the December party season. Pace yourself, there are more than three months to go and very little opportunity ever to catch up on lost sleep. By February, the days are longer and you are now into a fantastic rhythm. March arrives and you realise sadly that you only have weeks to go. If you've kept your chalet spotless from the start you will breeze through and work faster and more efficiently then you ever imagined . Don't slacken off towards the end, the March and April guests deserve as good a holiday as the earlier season ones.

End your season feeling proud that you have been a fantastic chalet host and helped the guests have amazing holidays.

INDEX

ALL IN ONE MUSHROOM SOUP	33
ANOTHER QUICK YOGURT CAKE	14
BAKED AUBERGINE MELTS	50
BAKED CAMEMBERT	38
BAKED CHICKEN OR FISH GOUJONS	29
BALSAMIC REDUCTION	60
BASIC SPONGE CAKES – VICTORIA, COFFEE AND BERRY	17
BEEF AND BEER PIE	42
BOULANGERE POTATOES	59
BREAKFAST QUANTITIES	7
BRIE EN CROUTE	38
BRUSCHETTA	39
BUTTERNUT SQUASH/PUMPKIN SOUP	32
CAESAR SALAD	64
CARAMELIZED BANANAS	70
CARAMELIZED ONIONS	61
CARROT CAKE	15
CELEBRATION NUT ROAST	56
CHEESE AND HAM POTATO BAKE	27
CHEESY EGGS	8
CHICKEN AND MUSHROOM PIE	42
CHICKEN STIR FRY	28
CHOCOLATE CHIP COOKIES	21
CHOCOLATE MUD CAKE	18
CHOCOLATE ORANGE MOUSSE	69
CHOCOLATE PEARS	70
CHOCOLATE SAUCE	70

CHRISTMAS GINGERBREAD	23
CHRISTMAS OR SPECIAL OCCASION SMOKED SALMON PATE	36
CLASSIC SKI CHALET YOGURT CAKE	14
COURGETTE, LIME AND POPPYSEED CAKE	16
COURGETTES WITH GINGER AND GARLIC SAUCE	53
CREAMY CHICKEN AND LEEKS	28
CREAMY ZUCCHINI SOUP	33
CRÈME BRULEE	67
CUSTARD	74
DAME BLANCHE	70
DAUGHINOISE POTATOES	59
DUCK CASSOULET	44
EGGS BENEDICT: FLORENTINE OR ROYALE	9
EGGY BREAD	12
EMERGENCY DESSERT	66
FISH PIE	48
FLAPJACKS	20
FLORENTINE SCRAMBLE	8
FOUR SEASONS SALAD	64
FROZEN FRUIT SORBET	72
FRUIT CRUMBLE	73
FRUIT TART	69
FRUIT TRIFLE	74
GF ORANGE/LEMON POLENTA CAKE	25
GF PASTRY	25
GF/DF COCONUT MACAROONS	24
GF/DF SPANISH ALMOND CAKE	24
GINGER COOKIES	22
GOAT'S CHEESE SALAD	65
GOAT'S CHEESE, WALNUT AND SUNDRIED TOMATO TART	37

GREEK SALAD	65
HASSELBACK POTATOES	59
HERB CRUSTED SALMON	49
HERBY CREAM CHEESE BALLS	36
ITALIAN BEEF CASSEROLE	47
ITALIAN STUFFED PEPPERS	50
JACKETS	27
LASAGNE	41
LCHF PANCAKES	12
LEMON TART	68
LEMON TUNA PATE	35
LENTIL AND VEGETABLE STEW	54
MEDITTERANEAN LAMB	46
MELBA TOAST	36
MINCE AND VEGETABLES PIE	43
MINCE PIES	23
MUSHROOM PANCAKES	51
MUSHROOM PATE	35
NICOISE SALAD	63
NUTTY RISSOLES	51
OMELETTES	10
PANNA COTTA	71
PARMESAN CHICKEN	45
PAVLOVA	66
PICANTE SAUCE	62
PORK FILLET MIGNON IN HONEY MUSTARD SAUCE	46
PORRIDGE	12
QUANTITIES OF VEGETABLES	57
RED PEPPER JAM	60

RED PEPPER SAUCE	61
ROAST VEGETABLE CASSOULET	52
ROASTED PEPPER, MOZZARELLA AND BASIL STUFFED CHICKEN	45
SCONES	20
SCRAMBLED EGGS	8
SHORTBREAD	22
SPEEDY MOUNTAIN FRUIT CAKE	19
SPICED BISCUITS	21
SPICED LENTIL AND TOMATO SOUP	34
SPINACH AND MUSHROOM LASAGNE	55
SPINACH SOUP	31
STICKY GINGER CHICKEN	44
STICKY TOFFEE PUDDING AND SAUCE	71
TARTIFLETTE	40
THICK PANCAKES/DROP SCONES	11
THIN PANCAKES	11
TIRAMISU	72
TUNA, BROCCOLI AND PASTA BAKE	29
VEGETABLE GRATIN	56
VEGETABLE SOUP	32
WAYS OF TARTING UP VEGETABLES	57
WILD MUSHROOM TARTIFLETTE	53
WILD MUSHROOM TARTS	37

Dev lives in Sussex and is married to Martin with two children Jacob and Naomi. As a teacher she learnt to cook and cater whilst working with disaffected adolescents in residential therapeutic settings. Following a ski season working in the Italian Dolomites in 1990, Dev has continued to work in the catered chalet business for over 25 years and has a passion for helping chalet hosts provide excellent holidays for their guests whilst having a fantastic chalet season themselves. When in the UK, Dev also loves demonstrating and teaching people to use the Thermomix, the best appliance available for kitchens.

Printed in Great Britain
by Amazon